I0796342

This journal belongs to

....

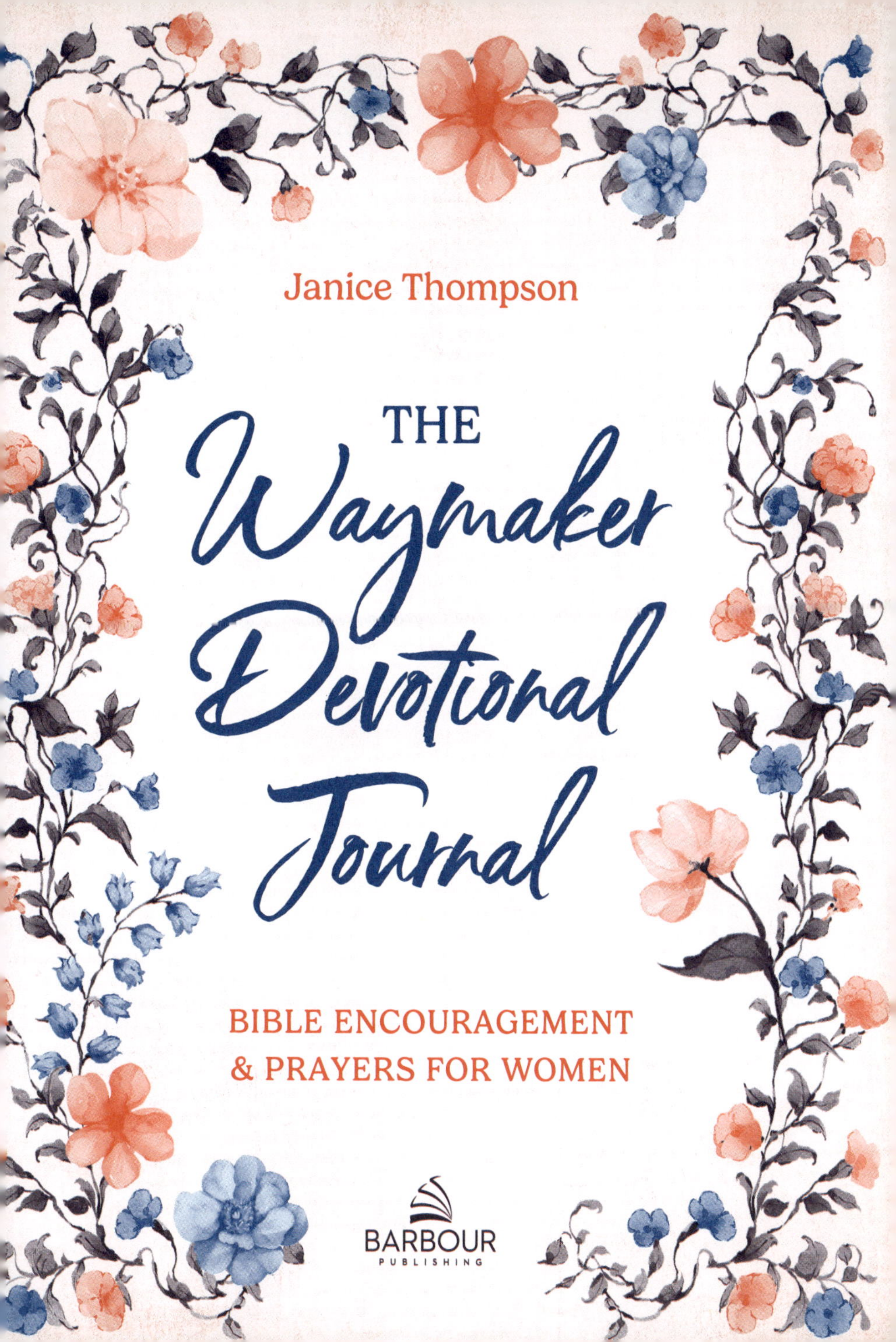
Janice Thompson
THE
Waymaker
Devotional
Journal
BIBLE ENCOURAGEMENT
& PRAYERS FOR WOMEN
BARBOUR
PUBLISHING

ISBN 979-8-89151-131-6

Text previously published as *God's Way through Brokenness*, published by Barbour Publishing, Inc.

Published by Barbour Publishing, Inc., 1810 Barbour Drive, Uhrichsville, Ohio 44683, www.barbourbooks.com

Our mission is to inspire the world with the life-changing message of the Bible.

Printed in China.

Nothing Is Impossible with God.

My sacrifice, O God, is a broken spirit; a broken and contrite heart you, God, will not despise.

PSALM 51:17 NIV

If you're like most women, you probably wonder why life is filled with so many broken moments. You look at them and say, "I can't possibly get beyond this horrible mess. The wounds are too deep to mend."

Lift your head, precious woman of faith! God is on the move even now, making a way through whatever you are facing. He has a holy superglue to mend every crack. No matter what has broken your heart—a betrayal from someone you thought you could trust, the sting of rejection from a child, the death of a loved one, a financial loss, or dashed hopes after being diagnosed with an illness—this journal is for you.

God is your Waymaker. He *will* make a way through the pain and brokenness. Even if your dreams have been shattered and you're crying out, "My heart can *never* mend from this," He'll step in and supernaturally fill those cracks and crevices, bringing healing to that broken heart once again.

Through these devotions, you will see that your Creator thrives on doing the impossible. He can do what you cannot! When you throw up your hands and say, "I can't!" He steps in and says, "Oh, but I can. . .and I will!"

A Broken Vessel

I have been forgotten like one who is dead;
I have become like a broken vessel.
PSALM 31:12 ESV

Have you ever tried to drink from a cup with a crack in it? When ceramics or glass vessels have even the tiniest hairline crack, the beverage leaks out, sometimes a few drops at a time, other times in a great gusher, until the crack turns into a full break.

Sometimes the world looks at those of us who aren't "perfect" (by their standards) like we're leaky, cracked cups. They don't place much value in us. We get tossed in the trash or pushed to the back of the cabinet.

Here's great news for you today: When God looks at you, He doesn't see you as broken at all. No matter your struggles. No matter your past. No matter your wrinkles or warts. He sees a woman who is whole, healed, and ready to be used by Him.

Don't allow the enemy of your soul to convince you that you're not usable. When you get discouraged or start to doubt your usability, think about Fanny Crosby, the great hymn writer. Blind from early childhood, she surely seemed "broken" by the world's standards; but she showed them! Through the power and anointing of the spirit of God, she went on to write hundreds of great hymns that we still sing today. One of the most powerful, "Blessed Assurance," is a great reminder that no matter how broken or flawed we are, the King of kings still loves and accepts us!

He will use you, precious woman of God, no matter how broken you are.

Lord, the world sees me as broken. I've looked at myself this way too. Thank You for the reminder that You don't see the cracks. You still find me worthy of love and usable. Thank You, Father! Amen.

He Will Not Despise You

The sacrifices of God are a broken spirit; a broken and contrite heart, O God, you will not despise.

Psalm 51:17 ESV

She pressed her way through the crowd, intent on reaching the Savior. When she finally got close enough, all the woman could do was stretch out her arm and pray she could touch the hem of His garment.

Finally! She had it within her grasp. A shockwave went through her as healing coursed through her veins. Was it really possible? Had her years of brokenness finally come to an end? And all with a simple touch?

The moment Jesus felt her touch, He stopped. He (literally) felt virtue leaving His body as the sick woman was healed. And when He did, His whole world stopped too. He called out, "Who touched me?" Then He searched the crowd until He found the one who had received supernatural healing.

That's a powerful story, isn't it? The woman with the issue of blood was despised by those around her but not by Jesus. Others were likely weary of hearing her complaining about the "same old same old." We don't mean to grow callous and unfeeling, but sometimes we do. We get weary with people who come to us with the same complaints. We consider them needy.

Jesus considers them needy too but in a completely different way. He looks at their brokenness, their need, and then reaches down in such a gentle and loving way to meet that person at the very point of that need. In other words, He cares. He cares far more than we ever could, and He's teaching us to do the same.

Lord, show us how to care as You care. May we not give up on those who are broken and hurting, no matter how "annoyed" we are at their complaints. May we never forget that You plan to make a way for all who come to You. Amen.

Come, My Child

Then Jesus said, "Come to me, all of you who are weary and carry heavy burdens, and I will give you rest. Take my yoke upon you. Let me teach you, because I am humble and gentle at heart, and you will find rest for your souls."

MATTHEW 11:28–29 NLT

If you've mothered children (or have nieces and nephews), you've likely been on hand to watch a baby take his first steps. There's something so precious about that letting go and trusting moment when he puts one foot in front of the other. Oh, and that delightful giggle as he realizes he's done it! He's actually upright and walking!

Question: When a child is toddling toward you for the first time, what are you doing? (Besides filming it, of course!) No doubt you have your arms extended in his direction, encouraging him to come straight to you. You're saying, "Come! Come on, sweetheart! Come to Mommy! (Or "Come to Grandma!" or "Come to Auntie!") You're encouraging him to take steps in your direction, and you're reassuring him with your tone that he will be safe on the journey.

God is like a wonderful, loving parent with His arms outstretched. He asks you to come not because He's looking for you to show off your steps but because He knows you're weary. He knows you're carrying a load too heavy to bear. And He's right there, arms extended, saying, "I've got this if you'll just bring it to Me."

Today, even if it's hard, take steps in His direction. Allow Him to catch you if you fall. Follow His tender voice and move confidently toward your Waymaker so that you might receive healing for all that is broken in your heart today.

Lord, I come! Weary, broken, and in need of healing, I come to You. I come with scars, with flaws, with imperfections. I come because I know I can trust You, my Waymaker! Amen.

He Makes a Way When You're Downcast

Why, my soul, are you downcast? Why so disturbed within me? Put your hope in God, for I will yet praise him, my Savior and my God.

Psalm 42:5 NIV

"I'm just in a slump lately. I can't seem to shake it."

Maybe you've heard those words from a friend or family member. Or maybe you've spoken them during a rough season when you felt ready to give up.

Think about the biblical story of Ruth and Naomi: a mother-in-law and daughter-in-law, both recently widowed and still grieving, left on their own to make their own way. Clearly distraught, worried, filled with questions, they wondered what would happen to them. But they stuck together. They went to Naomi's homeland, back to her people, and there—in that special place—God restored them both. It didn't happen overnight. In fact, Ruth had to work hard in the fields, gleaning wheat. In other words, she played a key role in her story's plotline. But, in the end, the Lord intervened. In fact, He intervened in a way that changed the course of history for the Jewish people. He led Ruth to a wonderful new husband. Their love story still inspires multitudes today.

God will change your broken story line too. He'll intervene and set things right. It might not look like what you anticipated. It will look better. That's how your Waymaker works. Even in the darkest situation, you can count on Him to point you toward a bright future.

No matter where you are today, don't give up. Think of Ruth and

Naomi. Put one foot in front of the other, and head back home to your Waymaker. He's longing to restore you even now.

Lord, I won't turn in any other direction. I'll come to You when I'm broken, hurting, and lost. I won't give in to fear or defeat. I'll trust You, just as Ruth and Naomi did. I can't wait to see how You're going to mend the broken places, Father. Amen.

He Lets Me Rest

The Lord *is my shepherd; I have all that I need. He lets me rest in green meadows; he leads me beside peaceful streams. He renews my strength. He guides me along right paths, bringing honor to his name.*

Psalm 23:1–3 NLT

No doubt you've read the Twenty-Third Psalm hundreds of times over the years. You know it by heart and even have your favorite key verses. But have you actually paused to think about what God is telling you through this familiar and comforting passage?

"He lets me rest in green meadows." Think about that for a moment. If you didn't have a PAUSE button, you would never rest. You'd just keep going and going and going. And though you might not have wanted a season of distress or pain, you've allowed God to use it to bring rest, which is one good outcome.

During those restful seasons, God leads you to good places—green pastures. Not dry, barren wastelands but lush, green pastures. The pasture is where sheep go to graze, to get sustenance. It's also a quiet place to inspire, to breathe new life. Your Waymaker leads you beside peaceful streams, where you will find cool, refreshing waters to restore your soul.

When you finally "pause" long enough, He's able to do what you rarely allow Him to do during those crazy-busy seasons. . .He renews your strength. He gives it back to you. Then, once you're renewed, you're better able to walk those "right paths" with His guidance.

When you put it all into perspective, it's easy to see that, if you let Him, God uses the broken, hard times to work a miracle that might never happen otherwise.

So, let Him.

You'll come out of this stronger, braver, and with greater vision for the future.

Lord, You've promised to make a way where there seems to be no way. I can't wait to see where You're going to lead me. I know I will find myself in greener pastures. You've promised to bring full restoration there. How blessed I am to be led by You! Amen.

Don't Consider It Strange

Dear friends, do not be surprised at the fiery ordeal that has come on you to test you, as though something strange were happening to you. But rejoice inasmuch as you participate in the sufferings of Christ, so that you may be overjoyed when his glory is revealed.

1 PETER 4:12–13 NIV

We're always so shocked when tragedies befall us or life is harder than we expected. Perhaps it's our "me-first" mentality that has convinced us we'll never suffer like others do. Or perhaps we've swallowed one sermon too many about how God wants us healthy, wealthy, and wise.

The truth is life isn't always easy. People aren't always wealthy. And there are occasional seasons of illness or pain.

Consider the story of Maximilian Kolbe, a Polish Franciscan priest. In 1941, at the height of Hitler's tyranny, Kolbe was arrested and sent to Auschwitz. His crime? Harboring and sheltering Jews. Instead of fighting to save himself (as any one of us would probably do), Kolbe did the unthinkable—he volunteered to take the place of another prisoner condemned to death. He died in another man's place.

Known as "the Saint of Auschwitz," Kolbe left his mark on humanity. God used him to make a way for another human being to have life. Kolbe used a season of unfairness and brokenness to leave a legacy greater than any he could have possibly had otherwise.

Believers have a greater calling, for sure. And these tough seasons, no matter how challenging, can propel us to be better people—stronger, better able to live sacrificially, and ready to face the hard seasons with an eternal perspective.

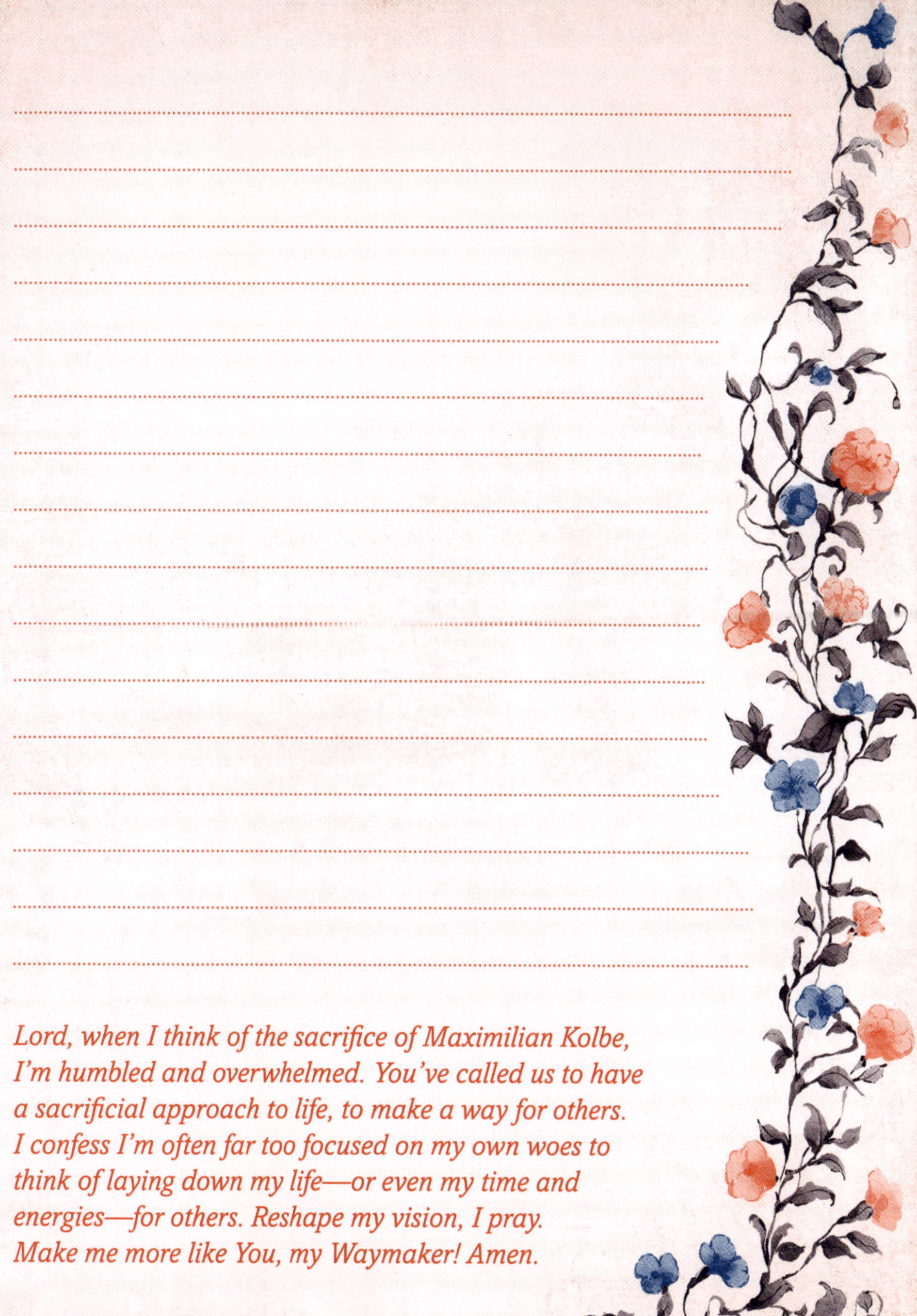

Lord, when I think of the sacrifice of Maximilian Kolbe, I'm humbled and overwhelmed. You've called us to have a sacrificial approach to life, to make a way for others. I confess I'm often far too focused on my own woes to think of laying down my life—or even my time and energies—for others. Reshape my vision, I pray. Make me more like You, my Waymaker! Amen.

Praise Your Way Through

Are any of you suffering hardships? You should pray.
Are any of you happy? You should sing praises.
JAMES 5:13 NLT

It seems impossible. What you're facing isn't fair, it isn't right, and you can't imagine how you should navigate it. The very last thing you feel like doing right now is singing a song of praise. And yet that's the very thing you should do!

Your Waymaker loves to work miracles on your behalf, but He's keen to have your participation even before you see the outcome! (Now that takes trust!)

Consider the story of Paul and Silas. Chained and imprisoned for preaching the gospel, they sat in a jail cell. This situation would probably make us feel pretty defeated, but not these guys! They decided to usher up praise.

In the midnight hour, in the very middle of their praise-a-thon, an earthquake hit! It rattled the place and broke their chains. It also swung wide the prison doors. Wow!

Their guard, thinking they would all escape, asked them to take his life. He knew his superiors would do him in if the prisoners were all gone in the morning! But Paul and Silas had another tactic. They shared the gospel with this man—their former captor—and within hours his whole household was saved!

God can do remarkable things even in our darkest moments. Whatever you're facing—whether it's literal chains or symbolic ones—don't allow your brokenness to keep you from praising! Use those "midnight hours" in a way that will lead to a miracle. Your Waymaker wants to include you in what He's about to do.

Thank You, my Waymaker, for involving me in the miraculous! I want to see prison doors swing wide in my life and the lives of those I love. Even now, in the midnight hour, I will lift up a song of praise for what You have yet to do. Amen.

A Heavenly Handkerchief

"'He will wipe every tear from their eyes. There will be no more death' or mourning or crying or pain, for the old order of things has passed away."

REVELATION 21:4 NIV

Can you picture the Lord leaning down with a tissue in hand to dry your eyes when you're weeping? A day is coming when every tear will be wiped away. Crying will cease. Death will be behind you. But right now, the pain is palpable. The grief seems unbearable. You wish it would end, but it doesn't seem to be getting better. . .and you're weary with the platitudes from those who simply don't understand. This is what it feels like to have a broken spirit.

Perhaps you recall the story of King David, who took another man's wife and then had her husband killed in battle. That wife—Bathsheba—went on to have a child who passed away. What a sad and complicated tale!

Much has been said about David's journey through that loss, but the Bible doesn't delve into Bathsheba's part of the story. Can you picture this story from her perspective? She has lost her first husband at the hands of her current husband and has now lost a baby boy. The devastation must have been more than she could take.

Maybe you've been in a situation where you were removed from your normal life and placed in another that you did not choose. Along the way, you experienced losses that seemed unfair. Cruel, even. And the platitudes from onlookers didn't help! Their "It's going to get better! Just trust God!" comments felt like acid on an open wound.

But then the Lord began to gently restore you. It happened slowly, gently. . .but it happened.

Bathsheba went on to have more children. God somehow redeemed the situation, but the loss of that precious baby boy never went away. He will birth new things in you too. And those well-meaning friends? Well, their words might have seemed like platitudes, but they were actually right. If you can put your trust in the Lord even now, He can work this situation for your good and for His glory.

I won't give up, Father. I know You want to birth new things in me. I'll trust You, my Waymaker. Amen.

It's Just a Sliver in Time

And after you have suffered a little while, the God of all grace, who has called you to his eternal glory in Christ, will himself restore, confirm, strengthen, and establish you.

1 PETER 5:10 ESV

It feels like forever. But years from now, when you look back on the rough seasons you've walked through, they will feel like a blip, a tiny sliver in the windows of time. The key is to treat them as non-eternals when you're walking through them.

If anyone understood this, it was Job. He was a man who had everything. Then, just as quickly, he had nothing. He lost his family, his home, his resources, and his health. Job did what so many of us might do in a similar situation. He curled up in a ball and felt like giving up. Even his close friends encouraged him to give up! (Who needs enemies when you have friends like that, right?)

But God wouldn't allow Job to lose all hope. When Job was at his very lowest point, when the situation seemed impossible, his Waymaker began to move.

By the time the story ended, all had been restored. God brought a new family, a new home, and great hope to Job's life. And He will do no less for you.

Yes, it might feel like forever. (It probably did to Job.) But you will look back on your seasons of loss and pain from a different point of view. They'll be in the rearview mirror. And a new season of restoration will bring hope—not just for today but for all of your tomorrows. The past will be a momentary blip in time.

You can trust Him, my friend. You can trust Him.

Lord, I do trust You, even while I'm waiting for You to move. If you could restore Job's situation, then I believe You can intervene in mine as well. I submit myself to the process even now. Amen.

Lean on Him, Not Yourself

Trust in the LORD with all your heart, and do not lean on your own understanding. In all your ways acknowledge him, and he will make straight your paths.

PROVERBS 3:5–6 ESV

Who do you lean on when the storms of life come barreling down on you? Your friends? Your own feelings or emotions? Maybe you've heard that old adage about a ladder only being as safe as the wall it's leaning against. That's true in your life too.

So, who are you leaning on? When you're walking through a season of brokenness, from where do you get your strength? From family members? From your friends? From a counselor? From a pastor?

Those are all good choices, but the Lord doesn't want you to forget that He's truly the only wall strong enough to support your ladder. He wants to be your first call. He wants to be your last call. (It's okay to call all those other people in between, of course.)

Ultimately, He has the answers. Others might have suggestions. They might have knee-jerk reactions to your situation. A few might be able to offer godly wisdom. But when it comes right down to it, your Waymaker is the only one who can make a way where there seems to be no way.

That's what you're needing, right? To get from point A to point B?

So, don't put your trust in people. And don't put it in your job, your bank account, or your own ingenuity. Those things all have the potential for failure. Instead, trust your Waymaker. Lean your ladder in His direction. He is strong enough to support you when no one else can. He won't let you down.

Lord, I've leaned on so many people in my lifetime. I thank You for the ones with wisdom who have always pointed me right back to You. Today I choose to lean my ladder against You, my Waymaker. You're strong enough to handle everything I'm going through, and I'm so grateful. Amen.

Shimmers of Light

Even when I walk through the darkest valley, I will not be afraid, for you are close beside me. Your rod and your staff protect and comfort me.

Psalm 23:4–5 NLT

Picture yourself walking through a deep, dark valley. You're so far down that ribbons of sunlight can barely reach you. Every now and again you catch a tiny glimpse of something that looks like light, but then it vanishes, and you're left to navigate the rocky, unfamiliar terrain in total darkness once again.

Mary and Martha went through a valley this dark. Their brother, Lazarus, died, and they didn't understand why their friend Jesus didn't come in time to save him. It seemed as though Jesus could have. . .but chose not to! Their grief was mixed with other emotions, along with an abundance of "Why, Lord? Why?" questions.

Why didn't God fix this?

Why didn't He intervene?

Why didn't He save my child, my parent, my home from foreclosure?

When you're deep in the valley, those "Why?" questions come in abundance.

Here's the truth: God always has a better plan. Jesus waited until Lazarus was "good and dead" and then performed a miracle that no one could ever dispute—He raised Lazarus up out of the grave!

Wow! Talk about a blast of light cutting through the darkness of Mary and Martha's valley!

And talk about a testimony for Lazarus, who—from that day forward—was known as "the man Jesus raised back to life."

He will raise you back to life too, so don't despair in the depths of the valley. He's going to break through in glorious splendor when the timing is right. And when He does, what a testimony you're going to have!

I trust You, my Waymaker. I trust Your timing. It's not easy to say that. Everything inside of me fights it. But I will wait on You, knowing that You have a far superior plan to anything I could come up with on my own. Amen.

Under His Wings

He who dwells in the shelter of the Most High will abide in the shadow of the Almighty. I will say to the Lord, "My refuge and my fortress, my God, in whom I trust."

Psalm 91:1–2 ESV

Remember, as a child, how you loved to walk with your mom's or dad's arm over your shoulder? There was something so comforting about tucking yourself into their embrace as you moved along. Your Waymaker wants you to tuck yourself under His wings so that you are safe. He's also longing to embrace you so that He can uplift and inspire you.

Consider the story of William Cushing, American minister and hymn writer. His wife passed away in 1870. Cushing was struggling with health issues, so he retired from the ministry. From the outside, people must have looked on and said, "Poor fellow. His best days are behind him."

But they weren't! Cushing continued to abide with the Lord. He tucked himself under Christ's wings; and in that precious, holy place, his Waymaker uplifted and inspired him. In fact, Cushing was so inspired that he started writing hymns. Perhaps you've heard a few of these: "Ring the Bells of Heaven," "Under His Wings," and "Hiding in Thee."

Do you notice a theme in those last two? Clearly, Cushing learned that "under His wings" was the place to be when you've walked through a deep valley. Tucking himself away was just what he needed.

Just when people felt sure his best days were in the rearview mirror, God proved them all wrong. He'll do the same for you. Your precious Waymaker wants you to know that your future is safe with Him. It's as solid as the ground you're standing on. If you tuck yourself under His wing, He will guide you where you need to go.

I will hide myself under Your wing, Lord! I need Your inspiration. I need Your protection. I need the reminder that my best days are still in front of me. Thank You for caring so much, Father! Amen.

I Need Your Protection

But as for me, afflicted and in pain—
may your salvation, God, protect me.
PSALM 69:29 NIV

Perhaps you've heard the name William Tyndale. This remarkable man of God lived in the fifteenth century and was one of the very first to print the Bible in English at a time when doing so was against the law. (Nothing like putting the Word into the hands of the people, right? This was a first for many believers: to have a Bible they could read for themselves.) To thank him for his "crime against the church," Tyndale was executed for blasphemy. It's hard to fathom such horrendous persecution against a fellow believer, but he literally sacrificed his life so that we could read the Bible in English.

Where would we be today, if not for the bravery of this lone man? Would the Word of God have made it into hands of commoners? Would we have the Word hidden deep in our hearts if Tyndale had not courageously given it to us? The world needs more men and women with the bravery of William Tyndale.

Following Jesus takes courage at times. Even now, as the world seems to be going crazy around us, we need to rely on the Lord's protection to see us through, especially as we find ourselves disagreeing with the upside-down narrative we're being presented. We are walking through a season of turmoil, persecution, and misunderstanding. If we speak up and say, "No, that's not right!" we're labeled and censored. Sometimes it feels as though the world has gone crazy!

But God. . .

Our Waymaker intervenes and protects us when we need it most. No matter what you're facing today, He is your guardian and friend, the one you should turn to. Place your trust wholly in Him and watch Him move!

Lord, I know I can trust You to guard and protect my heart and my body. I trust You with my life, Father! Amen.

Not Just Pieces

For I consider that the sufferings of this present time are not worth comparing with the glory that is to be revealed to us.
ROMANS 8:18 ESV

Have you ever been in a situation where you were willing to give God pieces of your heart but not all of it? Maybe you've been hurt in a particular area and just can't let go of that one nagging fear. Or maybe you've been unwilling to forgive a particular injury someone caused you. Now, every time you think about it, you close yourself off a little more.

Imagine you set out to bake a cake. You added the flour, the sugar, the butter, the milk, and the vanilla. But you left out the baking powder. It would still bake—sort of—but it wouldn't be the same, would it?

Now imagine a car shop putting the pieces of a car together. They do the body work, add the transmission, the fuel tank, and so on, but they leave out the engine. That car wouldn't even turn on.

Here's the truth: If you're going to do it, you need to fully do it. Give your whole heart to Him. Sure, God can piece things together for you, but how much better would it be if you were to go ahead and give Him everything?

What areas are you struggling in? Look past the shadows, beyond the cobwebs, way back to the recesses of your heart. Tucked away in the corner, you might just find that *one* thing you've never really been willing to give to Jesus.

He wants it all.

He can handle it all.

He will fix it all.

Lord, I know that I can trust You with the pieces that I haven't yet given You, but it's so hard. There are pains so deep, betrayals so staggering, that they've done serious damage. But I'll go past the shadows today, Father, because I know it will be worth it to be totally and completely healed. I trust You, my Waymaker, even in this. Amen.

Broken Promises

But you should keep a clear mind in every situation. Don't be afraid of suffering for the Lord. Work at telling others the Good News, and fully carry out the ministry God has given you.

2 TIMOTHY 4:5 NLT

Have you ever been the victim of a broken trust? Perhaps a parent promised you something and then didn't follow through. Or maybe a spouse broke your heart by violating a marital covenant. Broken promises can hurt. . .a lot.

In the book of Genesis, we read a story about a relationship between fraternal twins Jacob and Esau, sons of Isaac and Rebekah. Isaac loved Esau, the firstborn. Rebekah loved Jacob, their second son. When Rebekah hears her blind husband asking Esau for a bowl of savory venison stew, she flies into action and tells Jacob first. Jacob then dresses in Esau's clothes and covers his arms in animal skin (because Esau is a hairy man) and goes to his father, pretending to be Esau.

Isaac, not knowing the difference, passes on the firstborn's blessing to his second oldest. Can you imagine? The father was betrayed by his own son. And Esau was betrayed as well. He lost the blessing that should have been his. (And once given, that blessing couldn't be taken back.)

Esau, of course, is furious. He vows to kill his brother. Rebekah intervenes and saves Esau, but the damage has been done. The brothers have a falling-out.

Nothing hurts worse than the betrayal of someone you love, someone you thought you could trust. Some people never get past it. Others eventually forgive but spend years in bitterness or pain.

Maybe you've been there. If there's someone who hurt you, let today's message be the prompting you need to forgive. And if you've betrayed someone, your Waymaker is waiting for you to do what needs to be done.

Lord, I'm sorry for the times I've held others in unforgiveness and for the times I've broken the hearts of my loved ones. I truly repent. Show me how to make it right, I pray. Thank You for restoring trust and for mending relationships. Amen.

When There Seems to Be No Way

"Listen, Lord, to my prayer! My eyes are flooded with tears, as I pray to You. I am merely a stranger visiting in your home as my ancestors did."

Psalm 39:12 CEV

Women across the globe long for children. They do their best to smile and feign happiness when a friend announces a pregnancy, but many of them are broken and hurting inside. "Why not me?" they cry out in the quiet hours.

Hannah understood this cry. For years she struggled to conceive. Her husband had children with another woman, which only served to make things worse for Hannah. Would she ever be able to give him a child?

To complicate matters, Hannah—when pouring out her heart to God in the temple—was falsely accused by the priest of being drunk. This poor woman just couldn't catch a break.

Maybe you know what that feels like. Maybe you've been through IVF. . .and it didn't work. Maybe you've had well-meaning friends or loved ones say things like "Well, maybe you weren't meant to be a mom." Ouch! Don't they realize how awful that sounds?

Instead of pouring your energies into the accusations and/or inflammatory remarks, keep your focus on God. Hannah was blessed with a son, Samuel, and he went on to do amazing things for the country of Israel. All that she wanted, she received, but in God's time.

Your Waymaker will use this season of brokenness, sweet woman of God. He will turn it around and create a new narrative, one that will impact generations to come. So, don't give up. Keep on pouring out your heart to Him, just as Hannah did. Answers will come in His time.

Lord, You see my heart. You see my desires, my dreams for the future. Today I give them to You. I'm asking You to make a way where there seems to be no way. May You birth in me a new thing, Father! Amen.

No Lone Rangers

Carry each other's burdens, and in this way you will fulfill the law of Christ.
GALATIANS 6:2 NIV

Your Waymaker is always present, even when you can't feel Him. Whether you're sitting in a hospital bed, seated in a courtroom, or facing down an ex-spouse who is relentless in his goal to hurt you, Jesus is right there, not missing a thing. Even in the middle of all that brokenness, your ever-present God is doing what He does best: drawing close. And He's paying attention to every little detail. Nothing escapes Him.

What about you? Do you pay attention? Or do details escape you? You know what it's like: You're out to dinner with the kids, and they're telling you a story about something that happened at school, but you're busy thinking about something your boss said. Or maybe you're dealing with a string of text messages pouring through from the women's Bible study group you lead. The last thing you're doing is truly listening to that kiddo of yours.

Listen up, Mama. No, really. . .listen. Those kids need you. They're not able to handle the things they're going through on their own. And if you're not careful—if you don't pay attention in the moments when they're willing to open up and share—there may come a day when they stop trying.

God didn't create your children to walk alone. For that matter, He didn't create *anyone* to walk alone! The body of Christ was never meant to be made up of a bunch of Lone Rangers. If this were the case, then Paul would never have admonished us to bear one another's burdens.

When you're struggling, you need people.

When your children are struggling, they need people.

You're people.

They need you.

So, put down the phone. Set aside any worries or concerns about work. Be present with those children while they're willing to be present with you.

Lord, I want to pay attention so that I don't miss a thing. I want to be fully present with You and fully present with those I love. May they never doubt my love, I pray. Amen.

Courage in Impossible Situations

Persecuted, but not forsaken; struck down, but not destroyed.

2 CORINTHIANS 4:9 ESV

If you've studied the story of Dietrich Bonhoeffer, you know that he gave his life for the cause of Christ. A Lutheran pastor, Bonhoeffer was a critic of Hitler and Nazism. In 1943, Bonhoeffer was arrested for conspiring against the Nazi regime. He was a gifted and influential wordsmith, and his writings are still with us today.

Many would look at Bonhoeffer's story and say, "Wow, God really let him down. Think of the good he could have done had he lived."

We'll never know why his flame went out when it did, but this much we do know: Life is filled with stories that have unexpected, difficult endings. When we weigh those against the glory of eternity, though, the pain pales in comparison. What we learn from Bonhoeffer is this: Speak truth. As he said, "We are not to simply bandage the wounds of victims beneath the wheels of injustice, we are to drive a spoke into the wheel itself."

Bonhoeffer decided to be bold. He acted and used his platform for good, speaking truth and mincing no words. This godly man bravely stepped up as the lead spokesman for the "confessing church" (unrecognized by the state) and faced horrible opposition as a result.

Perhaps his life message was best summed up in these words: "Silence in the face of evil is itself evil: God will not hold us guiltless. Not to speak is to speak. Not to act is to act."

Bonhoeffer paid the ultimate price for speaking up. He was arrested and later executed in a concentration camp. But his memory lives on, and his role as a peacemaker is undeniable. If Christians hadn't taken a stand, where would the world be today?

Lord, I've been through so much. Many times, I haven't been brave. I haven't spoken up. Give me courage, even when everything seems to be against me, Father! Make a way, even when I'm terrified. Amen.

What Others Have

Many are the sorrows of the wicked, but steadfast love surrounds the one who trusts in the Lord.

Psalm 32:10 ESV

Jenny didn't think life was particularly fair. While she and her husband struggled to get by, friends soared to the top of the rung, financially speaking. They bought vacation homes, traveled abroad, went on cruises, and bought high-end, designer clothing. They posted about their exploits on social media. . .in between pedicures and dinners out with friends.

It wasn't that Jenny wanted all those same things. She just wanted to rest easy, to stop struggling over the monthly bills. To have school clothes for the kids and enough food in the pantry and freezer to last until the next payday, perhaps a bit longer. To know that they had a little cushion in the bank, should they need it. But no matter how hard she and her husband worked, they never seemed to catch up.

Maybe you can relate to Jenny's plight. It's hard not to be consumed with jealousy when your friends and loved ones seem to have it so easy and you're slaving away, working longer and longer hours. But if you take a closer look, you usually discover their stories are filled with other kinds of woes: relational issues, health issues, dissatisfaction, greed. The outward appearances can be deceiving.

Instead of fretting over what you don't have, today would be a great day to celebrate what you have been given. How many times has the Lord proven Himself to you? Too many to count! He's your Waymaker after all. So stop comparing! Thank Him for providing all you need and more.

Lord, I can trust You to make sure I have the provision I need. Help me with any feelings of inadequacy or jealousy, I pray. May I keep my sights on You and not on the "things" that others have. Amen.

Waking Up to a New Day

For thus says the One who is high and lifted up, who inhabits eternity, whose name is Holy: "I dwell in the high and holy place, and also with him who is of a contrite and lowly spirit, to revive the spirit of the lowly, and to revive the heart of the contrite."

Isaiah 57:15 ESV

Kinidy went through a long season of brokenness. An autoimmune disease tormented her and kept her in extreme pain. She tried to keep going, but after a while even getting out of bed was too much. Her husband took on the household tasks and tended to the children while she did her best to mend.

It didn't take long for Kinidy to give up. Psychologically. Emotionally. Spiritually. She felt abandoned by God, alone, and frightened. She went on for nearly a year like this—and even stopped going to church or hanging out with her Christian friends. Their words to her felt like empty platitudes.

One day she woke up. She couldn't put her finger on how or when it happened, but one morning she started feeling more hopeful. She took on a work-from-home job to bring in extra income, and spending time with the ladies on her team brought a new emotional energy. Before long, she was hosting parties on social media and surrounded by loving friends.

That's when the spiritual awakening began. God began to tug on her heart, and before long, she relinquished. She gave herself to Him afresh and even shared her heart-journey with her friends. Feeling better psychologically helped with the physical, and she soon felt like going back to church.

Maybe you've been there. Maybe you're there right now. Lean into the Lord and let Him minister to you. Don't give up. He will rouse you from your slumber and awaken you to many adventures ahead.

You are my Waymaker! You make a way past these feelings, even the ones I can't put my finger on. Then You wake me again, Lord. I'm so grateful when You do! Amen.

Chased to Be Chaste

And I am convinced that nothing can ever separate us from God's love. Neither death nor life, neither angels nor demons, neither our fears for today nor our worries about tomorrow—not even the powers of hell can separate us from God's love. No power in the sky above or in the earth below—indeed, nothing in all creation will ever be able to separate us from the love of God that is revealed in Christ Jesus our Lord.

Romans 8:38–39 NLT

She came into the marriage from a broken past—years of prostitution and abuse. And yet this man—Hosea—wanted her for his own. Gomer did her best to play the role of the chaste bride, but she found herself torn between the joy of her new life and the excitement of the past.

Out of nothing but longing for what she once knew, Gomer broke free and went back—to the men she had once known, to the life she had once lived.

And yet Hosea pursued her. He chased her down. He wooed her back home again. And he wouldn't take no for an answer, no matter how difficult she made it.

What a lovely picture this well-known Bible story paints! God is the best Hosea ever. He finds us in our sin, takes us as His bride, and gives us the best possible life. But, ever tempted, we find ourselves looking backward. We want the things we used to have, and so we begin to compromise, a step at a time.

But our new Husband isn't willing to give us up. His love for us runs deep. So, He chases us. He pursues us, pulling us from the deepest, darkest places. . .and all because He loves us.

Where are you in your Hosea story? Has God won your heart? Are you His forever? Or are you looking over your shoulder, wishing for your old life, the one where you were broken and lost? Remember, the lover of your soul won't be satisfied to let you go. Your Waymaker will chase you and woo you back with His tender love and care.

Lord, thank You for pursuing me! I don't ever want to go back to where I came from. I'm Yours. . .forever! Amen.

Here Am I. . .Send Me

In the year that King Uzziah died, I saw the Lord, high and exalted, seated on a throne; and the train of his robe filled the temple. Above him were seraphim, each with six wings: With two wings they covered their faces, with two they covered their feet, and with two they were flying. And they were calling to one another: "Holy, holy, holy is the Lord *Almighty; the whole earth is full of his glory."*

Isaiah 6:1–3 NIV

Don't you love worship services where the presence of God is so strong, so palpable, that you can literally sense that the Lord is right there with you? Can you even imagine what Isaiah must've been thinking? Talk about powerful!

An angel held a live coal and then touched it to the tip of Isaiah's tongue. In doing so, he blotted out Isaiah's sins.

The story picks up in verse 8: "Then I heard the voice of the Lord saying, 'Whom shall I send? And who will go for us?' And I said, 'Here am I. Send me!' "

This is where Isaiah really got it right! This visitation from God required something of him. He had to say, "Here am I, Lord. . .send me."

No matter where you are today or where you are in your journey with God, you can say, "I'm right here, Father. I'm ready, willing, and able."

You might be waiting for Him to use you in some big, amazing way. Today, there are three things the Lord wants you to know: He wants to meet with you, to blot out your past, and He wants a response from you. Perhaps this is the day you say, "Here am I, Lord. . .send me."

Lord, the remarkable encounters I have with You are meant to change me. I see that! You're waiting for a response from me. Today I come to you, arms extended, saying, "Here am I, my Waymaker. Send me." I don't have to know where or when (or even how). But use me as You will, Lord. Amen.

He Won't Leave You Now

Why is my pain unceasing, my wound incurable, refusing to be healed? Will you be to me like a deceitful brook, like waters that fail?

JEREMIAH 15:18 ESV

From the moment Annie got the news that her husband was leaving her for another woman, she locked herself away from other people. Even her own children had a hard time reaching her. She just couldn't seem to get past the pain his actions had caused.

Hadn't he promised to love her forever? Weren't they supposed to be together "till death do us part"? She had done her part—had offered him her best years, her best attempts at being a good wife, a good mom to his kids, and a good housekeeper in their home.

What excuse did he have to break her heart?

Here's the sad truth—the heartbreakers out there aren't looking for excuses. They don't usually hurt us because of anything we've done. They are most often selfish, motivated by their own lusts and desires. They're propelled by their wants and wishes and often give little thought to those they will hurt in the process of getting what they want.

Today, instead of asking all the "Why?" questions, focus on how God plans to sustain you through this season. He's the mender of broken hearts. He has a plan to get you to a place of healing. Your heart, tender as it might be, is capable of growing, changing, and mending. Don't give up on this one simple truth: God didn't bring you this far to leave you now.

You're my Waymaker! Yet I often forget that and start to wonder if You're going to leave me where I am. I'm so glad You're looking forward and have a plan for my future, Lord. Others might leave me, but You never will. How grateful I am for that promise, especially now. Amen.

Your Waymaker, Your Shield

But you, O Lord, are a shield about me,
my glory, and the lifter of my head.
Psalm 3:3 ESV

Have you ever seen a bulletproof vest up close? Many of the older ones were very heavy, made of strengthened steel plates. They could be cumbersome and difficult to maneuver in.

The latest technology uses lightweight composites of ceramic and titanium. These vests aren't as weighty, but they're still not the most comfortable thing in the world. (Picture having to wear it under a full uniform!) For the officer wearing the vest, however, the discomfort and added weight is a fair trade-off. The vest offers him added protection that could, in a pinch, save his life. And you'll notice that the most vulnerable organ in the body—the heart—is covered in full.

If a bad guy fired a round at the officer and a bullet hit him in the chest, the vest would disperse the round's energy and deform the slug, all in an attempt to minimize blunt force trauma. In a sense, a bulletproof vest would rob the bullet of its energy.

Think about that for a moment. The Bible says that God is a shield around you. He's your bulletproof vest, carefully guarding your heart. When the enemy slings his fiery darts your way, they're caught in that shield and dispersed so that only minimal damage can take place. And how remarkable to know that Satan is robbed of his energy in his attempts to take you down. That should bring you great comfort!

Here's a staggering truth: God, Himself, takes those bullets for you. He is your shield. You won't ever have to be fitted for a new one or require something stronger. Your Waymaker will never let you down. He knows when the enemy is ready to fire and is already on the job to protect your heart because He loves you.

Lord, thank You for covering and protecting me from the enemy's strategies and schemes. I know I'll be safe with You, my Waymaker. I'm humbled and honored by Your protection, Lord. Amen.

Equipped for Ministry

Praise be to the God and Father of our Lord Jesus Christ, the Father of compassion and the God of all comfort, who comforts us in all our troubles, so that we can comfort those in any trouble with the comfort we ourselves receive from God.

2 CORINTHIANS 1:3–4 NIV

It's common for people in ministry to struggle with feelings of inadequacy. Many think they're not qualified. They think, "Surely there's someone else who could do this job better."

One of the ways God prepares you for ministry is by allowing suffering in your life. How can you minister to others or understand the pain and suffering they are going through if you haven't been through rough times yourself?

The woman who's been through a divorce and is now healed and whole? She's the best possible person to minister to the one whose husband just left her.

That man who made it through two years of chemo? Who better to minister to the friend who's just been diagnosed?

That precious older lady who has lived for years on her own after the death of her husband? She's the best candidate to reach out to that young mom whose husband was just killed in a car accident.

Suffering equips.

It's just that simple, and it's just that complicated.

When you make it through the fiery trials of life—when you have experienced your Waymaker in the midst of them—your faith grows. As it blossoms and produces fruit, you're able to pass along the things you've learned to others who haven't learned them yet.

You have firsthand experience whether you want it or not. And now that you have it, you also have something else—a testimony. You are the best one to testify to God's sustaining grace and His plan for good in the lives of those who are struggling.

I'm not a fan of suffering, Lord. I'd like to avoid it at any cost. But when I see it as a part of my testimony, I realize that I am usable to others. Help me touch them, I pray. Amen.

No Memory Loss

"Can a mother forget the baby at her breast and have no compassion on the child she has borne? Though she may forget, I will not forget you!"

Isaiah 49:15 NIV

We're so forgetful sometimes. We walk away from situations and completely forget they happened. Don't believe it? Think back to your childhood. Do you have memories of every little detail? No; over time, those memories often fade away. Only when you look at photographs do you remember.

Moses struggled with memory loss. Though God had performed miracle after miracle for him, he needed a reminder to boost his faith. When he met with the Lord on Mount Sinai, God reminded him of how He had saved his people from the Egyptians and how He had parted the Red Sea. In fact, the Lord carried the Israelites on eagles' wings from the moment they left Egypt.

If God could remind you of the many times He's rescued you over the years, what stories would He tell? Which ones would He highlight? No doubt there are some miraculous tales waiting to be shared with friends who are walking similar paths.

Don't forget all that God has already done for you. Don't walk away from miraculous events and suffer memory loss. He wants you to remember so that your faith can be encouraged. Remembering His goodness will give you faith to believe that God hasn't changed. He's still good. He's still in the rescuing business.

Pause from your busy life long enough to encounter Him, as Moses encountered Him at Mount Sinai. Then, trust that He's going to come through for you again.

Hasn't He always?

Lord, I don't want to suffer from memory loss. May I never forget all You've done for me. May I always return to give thanks to You, my Waymaker. Amen.

The Right Word, the Right Moment

Anxiety weighs down the heart, but a kind word cheers it up.

PROVERBS 12:25 NIV

Just the right word at just the right moment.

Maybe someone spoke such a word into your life when you were in the depths of despair, when you thought no one noticed your pain. Like a shaft of light, it penetrated the darkness and gave you hope that all was not lost. Perhaps it came through a sermon or a song. Or maybe it came as a text or email from a loved one on a subject completely unrelated to your pain.

God uses these words from others often when you least expect them. And He uses you to speak timely words into the lives of loved ones who are trudging through seasons of brokenness.

Proverbs 25:11 (KJV) says: "A word fitly spoken is like apples of gold in pictures of silver."

How true! Such words can be lifelines for people in despair. And even when you're not in a crisis, a timely word is still much appreciated and can be planted deep in your heart for later.

Who needs a kind word from you today? That coworker who rarely treats you well? That elderly woman down the street who grumbles when you walk your dog near her property? That single mom who's struggling to get by?

Remember, just a word from you can serve as a life preserver if tossed at the correct moment. So, pray. Ask the Lord to show you who to minister to. Then be ready to act at His prompting.

Send a card. Bake some cookies. Shoot off a quick text. Do something to show that you care. Your words won't return void. They will provide just the hope your loved one needs at just the right moment.

Lord, I want to be a hope giver! I don't want to look past people in need. Give me words fitly spoken to share with those I love. . .and even those I haven't loved. May they be Your words, my Waymaker, not my own. Amen.

What a Friend We Have in Jesus

I can do all things through him who strengthens me.
PHILIPPIANS 4:13 ESV

Joseph Scriven is known for his beautiful hymns. Perhaps his most well-loved is "What a Friend We Have in Jesus." Understanding the backstory to this hymn puts the words in perspective.

Joseph experienced a great deal of tragedy in his life. The day before his wedding (when he was still a young man), his fiancée drowned. Can you imagine the devastation?

Years later, he dared to love again. This time he fell in love with a woman in North America. Sadly, she died of an illness before their wedding day.

Doesn't your heart just break for this young man? Two brides. Two catastrophic losses.

Instead of pulling inward, Scriven decided to take the opposite approach. He gave away his possessions and lived very humbly, serving others. That's often how it is with those who've lost a lot. They pare down even more, giving away anything that might serve as a distraction.

When Scriven heard that his mother was sick back home in Ireland, he wrote her a poem. He had no idea she would publish it anonymously, but that's exactly what she did. This poem became the familiar hymn we all know and love, but for years no one knew who wrote it!

When Scriven reached his golden years, he shared that he had written the poem that started it all. He wrote the words, "What a friend we have in Jesus, all our sins and griefs to bear. What a privilege to carry everything to God in prayer."

He, of all people, knew what it was like to bear griefs. But he also knew that Jesus—his Waymaker—was the one true friend he could turn to.

What about you? Have you struggled with untold griefs? Give them to your one true friend today. He will bear those griefs as you pour your heart out in prayer.

Lord, what a friend I have in You! Thank You for carrying my burdens and my pain. I will always turn to You, my one true friend. Amen.

Seasons of Betrayal

You keep him in perfect peace whose mind is stayed on you, because he trusts in you.

Isaiah 26:3 ESV

Have you ever placed your trust in a friend only to be disappointed by her in the end? Maybe she talked about you behind your back or wounded you in some other way. Perhaps she pretended to be a friend when you were together but said things about you that were spread around to others. Eventually, the gossip train got back to you, and you were heartbroken to hear all that had been said.

It hurts to be betrayed by a friend. It can break your heart and your spirit, especially when you've poured heart and soul into the relationship. Experiences like these can leave you wondering what you did wrong and how you can prevent something like this from happening again.

Perhaps it will bring you comfort to know that Jesus, the Savior of the world, felt the sting of betrayal from a friend too. Judas Iscariot, one of his twelve disciples, sold him out for thirty pieces of silver. Can you imagine? Judas took the money and ran. And because of the betrayal of this man, Jesus was arrested and then executed.

Friends might not always do right by us. They might stick proverbial knives in our back, but that doesn't mean we should give up on the concept of godly friendships. It is possible to love and be loved, to trust and be trusted.

No matter how badly you've been hurt or broken in this area, don't allow the enemy of your soul to discourage you or make you think you won't have solid friendships. You will. God has just the right people in mind for you, even now.

Lord, my heart has been broken by so-called friends. I've placed my trust in them only to be let down. But You? You're the best sort of friend! You'll never go behind my back or injure me. You're only looking out for my good. I know I can trust You to make a way, even through seasons when I've been betrayed. Amen.

He's Very Near

The L*ORD is near to the brokenhearted*
and saves the crushed in spirit.
PSALM 34:18 ESV

If you're like most women, there are seasons when God feels a million miles away. You tilt your eyes up to the ceiling as you pray and wonder, "Does He even hear me? And if He does, will He mend my brokenness? Will He really make a way even when there seems to be no way at all?"

God will not only mend your heart, He will restore you and bring you to emotional health again. He adores you. And here's the great news: He can see beyond today. He knows what's coming in all of your tomorrows. (He has eternal vision!)

Consider the story of Helen Roseveare. She was an English Christian missionary to the Congo in the mid-twentieth century, a trained medical worker. In 1964, Helen was taken prisoner by rebel forces. She remained their prisoner for five months, enduring the worst possible kinds of abuse. There seemed to be no way out of her situation. None whatsoever. Talk about feeling hopeless! This poor woman of God was completely broken down by her captors—body, soul, and spirit.

Then, miraculously, God made a way! Helen was released against all odds. God restored her and redeemed her life. She later returned to Africa to continue rebuilding the country.

If He made a way for Helen and restored all the broken pieces of her shattered and abused heart, do you think He will do any less for you? Your Waymaker adores you and has exciting plans for your life. You can trust Him, wholly and completely.

You will make a way, Father. I believe it! You'll mend the broken pieces of my life and restore me once again, just as You restored Helen. I will stand in faith and believe, even when those around me say it makes no sense at all. How I praise You! Amen.

A Hopeful Future

"For I know the plans I have for you," says the Lord.
"They are plans for good and not for disaster, to give you a future and a hope."
Jeremiah 29:11 NLT

Katie pushed back the tears as she loaded her personal items from her desk drawer to an empty box. The meeting with her boss had rocked her to the core, and the news that she was being fired was like a knife in the heart.

Why? What had she done to warrant this? She'd worked harder than anyone else on her floor, staying late and going above and beyond the call of duty. Of all people to fire!

Maybe you can relate. Perhaps you've been let go from a job where you've served diligently. The decision makes no sense to you.

God wants to remind you, during seasons like these, that He will use what the enemy intended for evil for good in your life. He can take anything, even an unfair job loss, and use it for His glory. He can lead you to a job where you'll be content and where your income level rises.

Best of all, He can plant you deep, among people who deserve you. Think of it this way: He's saving you for something much better!

The Lord has specific plans for you, and they are good plans. They're not for disaster, though it might seem like it in the moment. His plans are always to give you a future and hope.

So, let hope reign today, no matter what you're feeling. Your future is bright, girl!

Lord, I'm so glad You can see into the future and that You have wonderful things in store. It's easy to get stuck in the ruts. I'm grateful for the hope that only You can bring. Thank You for making a way even when things seem hopeless. Amen.

Pray. . .and Give Thanks!

Rejoice always, pray without ceasing, give thanks in all circumstances; for this is the will of God in Christ Jesus for you.

1 THESSALONIANS 5:16–18 ESV

Pray without ceasing. Always give thanks.

Jennifer did her best, but with her situation so precarious, she found it difficult. She was already working two jobs to make ends meet. Her youngest daughter was chronically ill, and her middle daughter struggled with serious learning disabilities. The oldest—nearly thirteen—was out of sorts lately. She wasn't acting like herself. And Jennifer's husband was so overwhelmed with a situation going on at his workplace that he seemed distracted and moody much of the time. Would he ever get the raise he needed so that they could finally stop working so hard?

Pray without ceasing. Always give thanks.

She repeated the words to herself and then began to do just that. Jennifer poured her heart out to the Lord, sharing her concerns and cares. Then the prayer took a twist, and she began to praise Him for the provision He'd already made and for the miracles yet to come. For the blessing of her children and her husband. For their jobs and for food on the table.

In the middle of the praise-a-thon, peace settled over her like a warm blanket. In that moment, she knew that everything would be okay. She just knew it.

Maybe you're in a similar situation. You don't really feel like praising just yet. Your miracle hasn't arrived, and you're wondering if it ever will. But here's a biblical truth—if you'll go ahead and praise Him now, the miracle will be all that much sweeter when it does come, because you will have played a role in it.

I choose to praise You now, my Waymaker! I won't wait until the answer comes. Your praise will continually be on my lips, even during the waiting seasons. Amen.

Confess. . . .and Receive

Is anyone among you sick? Let him call for the elders of the church, and let them pray over him, anointing him with oil in the name of the Lord. And the prayer of faith will save the one who is sick, and the Lord will raise him up. And if he has committed sins, he will be forgiven. Therefore, confess your sins to one another and pray for one another, that you may be healed. The prayer of a righteous person has great power as it is working.

JAMES 5:14–16 ESV

Why do you suppose the Bible instructs us to confess our sins to one another? Wouldn't it be easier just to deal with our own personal sins privately? Quietly? Why run the risk of word getting around by sharing it with someone else?

Here's the truth: Sharing your sin in confidence with a trustworthy friend is like opening the floodgates to peace and healing. Doing so also gives you an accountability partner, someone you can go to next time you're tempted in this area.

Mae learned this firsthand. While she was in the hospital with congestive heart failure, a couple of close friends showed up to pray for her. She let them anoint her with oil and start to pray, but in the middle of their prayers she became convicted over something she'd done years prior that she had never confessed to anyone. When she blurted out the words, "I had an affair!" they shocked even her. But once those floodgates busted wide, she was able to open up and confess the whole, ugly truth of what she'd done.

God didn't just begin the process of physically healing her heart that day; He also cleansed her from the sin and guilt of yesterday.

Where are you today? Is there anything you should confess? Ask God to show you a trustworthy friend who could listen and pray.

Lord, today I come to You asking not only for physical healing but for healing from my past as well. Thank You for forgiving me, Father, and for making a way where there seems to be no way! Amen.

Let It Be Done unto You

And my God will supply every need of yours according to his riches in glory in Christ Jesus.
PHILIPPIANS 4:19 ESV

Parents would do anything for their children. Climb mountains. Trek through valleys. Drive carpools. Sit at gymnastics practice. Anything.

There's a fascinating story in the seventh chapter of Mark about a mom from Tyre (modern-day Lebanon) who came to Jesus with a desperate plea. Her daughter was ill and in need of healing.

This woman was a Canaanite, a pagan. She wasn't Jewish and (by tradition) not someone who would have approached a Jewish man asking for anything. But that didn't stop this mama. Her daughter was broken and needed healing. This man Jesus could help her.

She cried out, "Have mercy on me, O Lord, Son of David!" These words show us that she had some knowledge of the Jewish messianic tradition.

Jesus didn't immediately respond to her. No doubt His disciples thought He was not interested, so they suggested He send her away. (She was annoying them with her cries after all!)

Though Jesus explained that He was sent for the lost sheep of Israel—the Jewish people—she just kept screaming, imploring, "Lord, help me!"

Jesus broke with tradition and healed her daughter. He said, "O woman, your faith is great; let it be done as you have requested."

Mamas know how to get things done, don't they? Who are you praying for today? Your Waymaker will meet your needs. . .and theirs. No doubt about it.

Lord, thank You for meeting not just my needs but the needs of those I love! Make a way for the people I care so much about, I pray. Amen.

Trust Him, Not Yourself

For we do not want you to be unaware, brothers, of the affliction we experienced in Asia. For we were so utterly burdened beyond our strength that we despaired of life itself. Indeed, we felt that we had received the sentence of death. But that was to make us rely not on ourselves but on God who raises the dead. He delivered us from such a deadly peril, and he will deliver us. On him we have set our hope that he will deliver us again.

2 CORINTHIANS 1:8–10 ESV

Are you in a post-affliction era? Maybe you've been through a recent shaking, and it has left you feeling discombobulated. You somehow make it through each day, but things aren't the same. You're just a shell of your former self. That shaking really took the energy and the want-to out of you.

Today, God longs to remind you that He wants you to be more than a broken shell. Seasons of despair and grief will come, yes. But there is life on the other side of them, and He wants you to experience it even now.

Don't rely on yourself. Don't trust your own feelings. Remember, the Bible says the human heart is deceitful above all things. You can't depend on it—on good days or bad. But you *can* trust your Waymaker. He never changes. And His heart for you is proven and true. Has He ever let you down?

Think of the many times He's delivered you from the perils of the past. He will do it again. And God's version of deliverance is more than "drowning your sorrows in an online streaming service while eating rocky road ice cream." His version looks like blue skies and an ocean of possibilities.

You're my trustworthy Waymaker! You've never let me down, Lord. How could I ever doubt You? Thank You for always teaching me to rely on You and not on my own heart. Amen.

Spare Her. . .Please!

Yet it was our weaknesses he carried; it was our sorrows that weighed him down. And we thought his troubles were a punishment from God, a punishment for his own sins! But he was pierced for our rebellion, crushed for our sins. He was beaten so we could be whole. He was whipped so we could be healed.

Isaiah 53:4–5 NLT

Imagine you robbed a bank. No, really. Try to picture it in your mind. Now envision this: A random woman who happened to be in the bank at the same time came to your trial and said, "Please don't punish this woman! I was there. I saw her desperation. I saw her brokenness. Please let me serve her prison time for her!"

Let's assume you were already feeling pretty guilty about what you'd done. But this? This would send you right over the edge! To think that someone you had hurt with your foolish and selfish actions would actually want to take the punishment for your crime? Unthinkable!

In essence, that's what Jesus did. He saw your sin. He saw your rebellion. He saw your selfishness. All of that broke His heart. But He still said, "Let me take her sin and shame, Father. Let me pay the price so that she doesn't have to. I want to go so she doesn't have to. Spare her, please."

Wow! What a gift the Savior gave! Doesn't it humble you to realize He loved you so much that He was willing to give His very life for you? Do you see how much love He must have? He saw you in your brokenness, your sin, your shame. And He took all of that and turned it into the loveliest gift anyone could ever give—the opportunity to experience "forever" with Him.

Lord, I can never thank You enough! You saw how broken I was! You saw how out of control my life had become. And You still stepped in and took my sin, my precious Waymaker! You made a way for me to spend eternity with You. Oh, how I praise You for the love and forgiveness You poured out on Calvary! Amen.

He Meets You in the Pit

"But I say to you, Love your enemies and pray for those who persecute you."
MATTHEW 5:44 ESV

Joseph, the youngest of twelve brothers, found himself in the bottom of a deep pit. Not an emotional pit (though he'd probably hit rock bottom emotionally too). No, this was a literal pit, one his older brothers had thrown him into! Can you imagine your own loved ones disposing of you so easily? They were jealous of him because he shared a dream he'd had about how one day they would all bow down to him.

The story didn't end there. Those same brothers sold Joseph into slavery and then lied to their father, telling him that Joseph had been mauled to death by a wild animal. Joseph found himself in Egypt, and his story took several twists and turns. In the end, he worked his way up to a job at the palace. And just as he had dreamed, his brothers ended up bowing down to him.

Maybe you've never been thrown into a literal pit, but you know what it feels like to be ostracized, pushed aside by those you love. They've hurt you—with their words, their attitudes, their selfishness. And you've never been anything but good to them.

There, in that pit of brokenness and pain, God can meet you just as He met Joseph. He can pull you out and give you a completely different situation. It might mean separation from those you love for a season, but He always redeems—in His own way and His own time.

God is present. Even in the pit. He hears every word. He feels every sigh. He sees and feels every tear. His presence means He's present—totally, fully, wholly. And He will show you how to forgive those who put you there. You can rise from that pit healed of any pain they might have caused, once and for all.

Your Waymaker will make a way. . .from the depths back into the light.

Lord, I've been in some pretty deep pits! Some were of my own digging. Others were from the pain caused by people I once trusted. But You've always pulled me out! You reach down, gently lift me from the depths, and place my feet in a new, safe place. How grateful I am, my Waymaker! Amen.

Someone to Talk To

Therefore, confess your sins to one another and pray for one another, that you may be healed. The prayer of a righteous person has great power as it is working.
JAMES 5:16 ESV

Julia loved her best friend, Emily. They were confidantes, sharing pretty much everything. She loved the fact that she could go to Emily with all her concerns—even sharing her deepest, darkest secrets—and her words would be safe. Emily would pray but would never betray her by telling anyone else what Julia was going through.

It's hard to find friends like that, isn't it? But when you're in a season of brokenness, it helps so much to find a confidante, someone who is strong in the Spirit and strong in the Word. A friend like this won't let you stay down in the dumps for long, but she also won't make you feel guilty when you're having a rough day. This precious gal has conquered the art of balance—knowing when to speak and when not to. When to advise and when to hold back. When to scold (c'mon, you know you need it sometimes!) and when to wrap you in her arms.

When she does take the time to speak, her carefully thought-out words are like gold to you. How grateful you are to have her in your life!

Of course, it's also good to *be* a friend like that. You can't draw intimately close to just everyone, of course, but there might be one or two who could depend on you as they walk through a crisis.

God made us to bless each other in good times and in bad. So, keep your eyes wide open today. Who's struggling? Who needs someone to talk to? Be there for her and, in turn, she will be there for you. In the end, you'll both be stronger for it.

Lord, I'm so grateful for the friends who know just what to say when I'm going through a rough patch. It helps so much to have someone to talk to. Help me be that kind of friend to others, I pray. Amen.

Too Messy to Clean

He gives power to the faint, and to him who has no might he increases strength.

ISAIAH 40:29 ESV

Sharen stared at her messy garage and groaned. It looked like something out of a *Hoarders* episode. For years, the junk had been piling up. Empty boxes. Bagged clothes that needed to go to the resale shop. Christmas décor. Boxes of dishes she no longer used. What a mess! Now things had reached the point where she could barely fit her car inside the garage. Talk about embarrassing!

Her neighbor didn't seem to have that problem. Every time he opened the garage door, Sharen experienced garage envy. In his tidy space, everything was perfectly organized. Even the walls and concrete floor had fresh paint. She wondered if she could ever get her own garage to look reasonably clean.

"Rome wasn't built in a day," she said to herself. Then she began to break down the boxes that filled one corner of the garage. The next day, she tackled the junk pile in a different corner. The following day, her tools. She continued to work, day after day, until—at last—enough space had been cleared. As a bonus, she found enough items to warrant a garage sale, which brought in more than two hundred dollars.

Maybe you are like Sharen. You have a few messes. You feel like your space can't be used for its intended purpose. Or maybe you feel that way about yourself. You think your life is too messy, too far gone to ever reclaim your rightful purpose.

God wants you to know today that He's a whiz at cleaning things up! No matter how big the mess, no matter how far gone you might think you are,

He's willing to dive right in and set you on a clean path once more.

I trust You, my Waymaker, to do what I cannot!
Help me clean up this mess I've made, Father! Amen.

I Have Been Crucified with Christ

I have been crucified with Christ. It is no longer I who live, but Christ who lives in me. And the life I now live in the flesh I live by faith in the Son of God, who loved me and gave himself for me.

GALATIANS 2:20 ESV

It's hard to think about the details of Jesus' crucifixion without getting emotional, isn't it? If you saw the movie *The Passion of the Christ*, you came face-to-face with the reality of His sacrifice. It's overwhelming. It's humbling. And it causes such a sense of gratitude that you can hardly bear it. All for you.

When you think of laying down your life, what comes to mind? In today's verse the apostle Paul says, "I have been crucified with Christ." Exactly what does that mean?

Coming to Christ means laying down your life. It means trading your plans for His, trading your dreams for the bigger dreams He has for you. It means sacrifice, but it also means great joy, tremendous possibilities, and thrilling adventures you never could have dreamed up yourself!

When you walk through hard seasons, you think, "This is it. This is the crucifixion Paul was talking about." But it's not. The biblical version of crucifixion would never be for your pain. It would always be for your good. . .and for His glory.

No matter what you're walking through, the life you now live is meant to be lived by faith. It's an adventure meant to be fully explored and lived out. Why? Because you're fully cognizant of all that the Son of God did for you. His free gift of eternal life propels you to enjoy life to the fullest.

Lord, how can I ever thank You for what You did for me on the cross? I can't bear to think of the pain, but You were thinking of me and making a way for me to spend eternity with You. How I praise You for this precious gift! Amen.

It's All About Perspective

And Abram believed the Lord, *and the* Lord *counted him as righteous because of his faith.*
Genesis 15:6 NLT

Elizabeth often bemoaned the fact that her townhome was so small. Recently widowed, there was little she could afford. And as one entering her golden years, why did she need a big house, anyway? It made no sense.

Still, she struggled with envy from time to time as she watched her friends host parties in their big, beautiful homes. They seemed to have all the things she did not and plenty of space to put those beautiful things! She struggled to fit her belongings into her little home.

One thing brought comfort and joy. In Elizabeth's neighborhood, there was a small lake near a park. She would take her dog, Ziggy, for walks along the edge of the water. There, in that peaceful, beautiful place, everything came into perspective. She learned to give thanks to God for planting her in this neighborhood with such a gorgeous place to spend quiet time with Him.

It's all about perspective, isn't it? When we've been through seasons of loss, we hyperfocus on what we used to have and not what's in front of us right now. It's time to shift your focus and see the beauty that God has placed around you right here, right now.

Today, make a list of the things you're most grateful for. You might say, "my new kitchen faucet" or "a working car." When you really stop to look, you'll find that your life is filled with wonderful blessings from a Waymaker who cares about your needs.

Lord, thank You for the reminder that I'm already blessed. . . by the best! I don't need a bigger house, a nicer car, or fine things. I'm so grateful for what You've already provided, Father! You've given me everything I need and more, and I praise You for caring so much about me. Amen.

The Master Artist Is at Work

Cast your cares on the Lord and he will sustain you;
he will never let the righteous be shaken.
Psalm 55:22 NIV

Imagine you're out for an early morning walk with your dog. You happen to notice that your neighbor has already put out her trash. There, next to the trash can, sits a gorgeous lamp. You can't imagine why she's thrown it out. The base of the lamp is made of stained glass in multiple colors, now sparkling under the overhead rays of sunlight. And that shade! Gorgeous! That color would go perfectly in your living room, but. . .do you dare?

Then again, she did toss it to the curb, so why not?

You glance around, wondering if anyone is watching you. No. So, you pick up the lamp to give it a closer look. Only when you turn it around do you realize that a chunk of the stained glass is missing. Ugh. How dreadful to have such a thing of value go to waste simply because of an unexpected break.

Here's the beautiful truth—God takes broken things and puts them back together, even when they seem beyond repair. In the same way a skilled artist might take that lamp and add more stained glass, God can take the smashed, chipped parts of your life and seamlessly fasten them one to the other, making them as beautiful as ever.

Things of value—like you—are worth it. The master artist takes them gently in hand and does a marvelous work, making you even more valuable and authentic than before.

Never consider yourself a worthless piece of trash on the side of the road. When your heavenly Father looks at you, He sees a masterpiece!

Thank You, my Waymaker, for putting the broken pieces of my life back together. When I thought I was totally without value, You reached down and did a work in me that re-created me and reminded me that I am precious in Your sight. How I praise You! Amen.

Help from the Sanctuary

May the L*ORD* *answer you when you are in distress; may the name of the God of Jacob protect you. May he send you help from the sanctuary and grant you support from Zion.*

PSALM 20:1–2 NIV

When Lyn's father died, she went into a deep depression. Weeks prior to his death, her best friend turned on her, falsely accusing her of something she hadn't done. Even after proving her innocence, the relationship could not be saved.

Then, in the middle of all that, a bogus contractor took advantage of her, costing multiplied thousands and resulting in headaches.

When her father passed, it was all Lyn could do not to completely lose it. She curled up in bed, covers pulled to her chin, tears flowing. Her little dachshund sensed her pain. He snuggled up next to her and put his head in her lap. Then he did something that startled her. . .he climbed up on top of her and licked her tears away.

She didn't know whether to scold him or praise him, to be honest. But his affectionate response to her pain touched her heart. . .deeply.

Maybe you've been there. You struggled with deep pain. Then the Lord used a pet—a dog, a cat, a bird—to touch you in a special way. Having that sweet animal to cuddle, to hug, did wonders for your broken heart.

Take a look at today's verse, particularly this phrase: "May he send you help from the sanctuary." God knows what you need when you need it. And He thought you needed that precious pet, so he sent you help. . .with four paws. . .straight from the sanctuary!

How wonderful that He provided that precious friend for such a time as this.

Lord, I don't take it lightly that all of nature hears Your voice and responds. Thank You for these precious pets. They bless us when we're hurting and provide a source of comfort that only they can bring. Amen.

Are You Stressed Out? (Good!)

For our light and momentary troubles are achieving for us an eternal glory that far outweighs them all.

2 CORINTHIANS 4:17 NIV

Perhaps you've heard of the word *eustress*. Whenever you work out, you place stress on your muscles. It's hard when you're first starting out, but that eustress (which is a good thing) eventually whips those muscles into shape. Before long, you're lunging deeper, running farther, and bench-pressing heavier weight because you took the time to "grow" those muscles.

Sounds great, right? But here's a hard truth: No one wants to go through stressful seasons. It's true! They're never fun in the moment, and you're hard-pressed to believe they'll be worth it in the end. But when you see the outcome (greater strength, stronger mind and body), you realize it was worth the pain. You're leaner, tougher, and readier to take on even more challenges. Oh, I know you don't feel like it today, but after those muscles are a little more developed, you will. And remember, God is growing you into the woman you'll one day become. Don't fight the process or you might not grow as strong as you'll need to be!

Look at today's verse: "For our light and momentary troubles are achieving for us an eternal glory that far outweighs them all." You can't control the stresses of life that come against you. Those seasons are difficult, and you wish you could skip them altogether. But when you think of them as opportunities for eustress to take place, your perspective changes. Suddenly those "light and momentary" troubles are worth it because they're growing you into a mighty woman of God.

Look at those muscles, girl!

Lord, You're making a way past this stress, but in the meantime, You're strengthening me, growing me into a strong, powerful woman of God. While I'm here, use this eustress to make me more like You, my precious Waymaker. Amen.

Jesus with Skin On

And the scripture was fulfilled that says, "Abraham believed God, and it was credited to him as righteousness," and he was called God's friend. You see that a person is considered righteous by what they do and not by faith alone.

James 2:23–24 NIV

Nadia thought no one was paying attention. She poured out her complaints on social media, but few people responded these days. She texted her grown kids, but they all had jobs and families and didn't always get back to her for a day or two. When they did, their responses were typically just a sentence or two.

Dealing with a chronic illness had turned her into something of a whiner, but she couldn't seem to stop it. The ongoing pain was more than she could bear at times. Sometimes she felt like she was living only half a life not a whole one.

Then God stepped in and brought a couple of terrific friends. They texted regularly "just to check in." They offered to bring meals on hard days. These precious friends sent gift cards to local restaurants when she couldn't get out. And when she could get out, they picked her up and took her to lunch. Or dinner. Or a movie. These friends were a lifeline to her—Jesus with skin on, as some would call it.

Maybe you know what that's like. In your toughest season, you've wondered if anyone was paying attention. Did they care? Really? Then, from out of the blue, you got that text. Or that email. Or that phone call.

Maybe it's time to be that friend for someone else. Send a gift card. Drop a note in the mail. Text an uplifting scripture. Be Jesus with skin on.

You made a way by sending me friends, Lord! May I be that kind of friend to others. Give me creative ideas so that I can bless them, in Your name! Amen.

Mended Bones

He heals the brokenhearted and binds up their wounds.

Psalm 147:3 NIV

It was a simple accident. Dorothy simply missed the bottom step of the stairway. The next thing she knew, she was spread out on the ground below, her ankle twisted in a horrible direction.

The diagnosis was worse than she imagined—five broken bones: tibia, fibula, and three smaller bones in her foot. The doctor couldn't perform surgery until the swelling went down but needed to temporarily set the bigger bones so that they wouldn't begin to mend in the wrong position. With the help of some good pain medication, the procedure was completed, and Dorothy was scheduled for surgery three days out.

That's what happens to us sometimes. We go through seasons of brokenness. Then, instead of allowing our Waymaker to "set" the break, we forge ahead, allowing the fracture to heal without getting the proper alignment. The bones begin to knit together in an awkward way, and before long, we're a twisted mess.

Alignment isn't easy. But when you're already broken—when that marriage has ended or the home is being foreclosed on—the timing is always right to get things in order. Otherwise, you'll get stuck in the wrong position as time goes on.

God is the great mender. He majestically designed the human body to heal itself in miraculous fashion. His goal is always to see you knitted back together in a healthy way. Whether it's a physical break or a psychological one, your Waymaker has already made provision for you so that healing can come.

Lord, thank You for mending the broken places inside of me. Like broken bones are knit back together, You bring things into alignment in my life, even through the pain. I praise You, my Waymaker! Amen.

He Turns Broken Stories Around

Praise be to the God and Father of our Lord Jesus Christ,
the Father of compassion and the God of all comfort,
who comforts us in all our troubles, so that we can comfort those
in any trouble with the comfort we ourselves receive from God.

2 CORINTHIANS 1:3–4 NIV

Leonardo da Vinci was, perhaps, the most brilliant artist ever to live. He had no formal academic training but was a true Renaissance man. He went on to paint the *Mona Lisa*, *The Last Supper*, and many other remarkable works. He was also an inventor and is still revered for his technological ingenuity. People around the globe know his name and flock to galleries to see his work.

Leonardo's story didn't begin with such accolades. He was born out of wedlock to a poor peasant woman. In the beginning, it must have seemed that he was destined for poverty and a life of judgment from others as a result of a situation that was beyond his control.

God is in the business of turning broken stories like this around, though, and that's just what He did in Leonardo's life. He took a young man from a broken situation and propelled him into the spotlight not just in his generation but for centuries to come. Instead of judgment, he received praise. Instead of poverty, he received income for his art.

No matter where you come from, no matter how broken your past, your Waymaker will make a way. He will help you develop your gifts and use them for Him. He'll turn you into a real Renaissance woman, led by His Spirit, if you will allow Him to. And you will impact this world for the kingdom of God as you dedicate those gifts to the Lord.

Lord, I'm so grateful You don't judge us based on where we came from. There are things in my past I'd rather leave in the past. Thank You for stirring up the gifts You've placed inside of me. I want to use them for You, my Waymaker! Amen.

Scarred. . .on Purpose

You need to persevere so that when you have done the will of God, you will receive what he has promised.

Hebrews 10:36 NIV

When a farmer sets out to plant his flower seeds, he examines them carefully. Many varieties have tough seed coats. God designed them this way on purpose so that they wouldn't sprout too soon.

To get these "tough seeds" ready for planting, the farmer scars them, scraping and scratching them. Then he soaks them in water until they moisten and become pliable.

That sounds painful, right? It also sounds familiar. We go through seasons where we're scarred and scraped, and we think the pain is too great. But God puts us through a saturation process then plants us deep in His soil, and we grow into strong, healthy women.

It's not easy to go through a scarification season, but the Lord will use it to grow you like a beautiful flower, completely healed and whole.

Don't believe it? He did this for Cathy, who grew up in a household with an abusive, alcoholic father. She put up walls that were so tall, so thick, no one could break through. She hardened her heart and refused to let anyone in.

When she started dating in college, her boyfriend wondered why she shut herself off from him. It took time for God to soften that heart of hers and to bring total healing. But eventually her heart softened, and those walls came down. God "scarified" her and planted her deep so that she could finally grow.

Lord, the "scarification" process sounds so painful. But I know You will use it for my good. Get my heart ready, Father! Bring down any walls I might have put up. I want to be soft and pliable so that I can live up to my full potential. Thank You for the work You are doing! Amen.

A Better Life

"But the Helper, the Holy Spirit, whom the Father will send in my name, he will teach you all things and bring to your remembrance all that I have said to you."
JOHN 14:26 ESV

Patti wanted to give her children a life that was better than what she had growing up. Unfortunately, she married a man much like her father—manipulative and emotionally abusive—and her children ended up having a tumultuous home life too. She hadn't meant to repeat the pattern. In fact, Patti hadn't even noticed her husband's tendencies until long after they were married. But the children eventually suffered through the trauma of a broken home, just as she had. And their broken hearts were just as fragile as hers.

Patti told a friend in confidence that she felt like a twice-baked potato because she'd been through the same experience on two separate occasions. Was this to be her lot in life? Manipulating? Gaslighting? Pain?

Maybe you can relate to Patti's sadness. Your children have suffered, and you feel like you're to blame. You should have done more. You should have been more. You should have noticed more.

We all want ideal lives for our kids, but it should bring comfort to know that the same Waymaker who has seen you through is there for your kids. He's big enough, loving enough, and tender enough to reach them right where they are.

You can't mend this for them, but you know someone who can. And He's right there, already working on their behalf. Your Waymaker hasn't forgotten your pain, either. When He goes to work on a family, He desires to see every single person healed and whole.

Lord, I'm so grateful I can trust my children to You. I wanted to guard them from pain, but they've experienced it anyway. Guide them through it, I pray, my precious Waymaker. Amen.

The Potter's Wheel

The word that came to Jeremiah from the Lord: "Arise, and go down to the potter's house, and there I will let you hear my words." So I went down to the potter's house, and there he was working at his wheel. And the vessel he was making of clay was spoiled in the potter's hand, and he reworked it into another vessel, as it seemed good to the potter to do.

Jeremiah 18:1–4 esv

Have you ever been convinced you knew God's plan for your life? Then, suddenly, the plan shifted, and you had absolutely no idea where you were headed.

It happens.

Your vision becomes cloudy, confusion sets in, and you begin to wonder if you can really trust your Waymaker after all.

Here's the good news for those of us who place our trust in the Lord. He can take a broken plan and rework it into something new and beautiful. He can help you begin again after a broken marriage. He can craft you into a new woman after you've felt hopeless and useless. He can even work something beautiful out of a great loss like the foreclosure of your home or repossession of your car.

The point is the potter can take the vessel and make it something new. You might feel useless in His hands, but He's capable of reworking the hardened bits of clay and forming them into something exquisite, provided you stay soft and pliable. So, don't give up on Him and don't give up on you! One day you'll look back on this season and be glad you allowed Him to keep shaping you into the woman you were intended to become.

Lord, I know what it feels like to be on the potter's wheel. You've reshaped and remolded me many times over now! There have been hard seasons, but You've made a way through every one of them, often "growing" and shaping me as things progressed. How grateful I am for Your great love and care, my Waymaker! Amen.

Made Perfect by Suffering

For it was fitting that he, for whom and by whom all things exist, in bringing many sons to glory, should make the founder of their salvation perfect through suffering.

Hebrews 2:10 ESV

Jesus was made perfect by suffering. Stop to think about that for a moment. If He hadn't suffered, if He hadn't carried the weight of our sins on that cross up to Calvary, His story would not have been complete. He went through all the pain and agony out of His great love for us. And the Bible says that it was "fitting" that He should suffer.

We don't like to think of suffering that way, do we? It doesn't seem fitting at all—not for us and certainly not for Jesus, who never sinned. And yet God seems to think that suffering can be woven seamlessly into our story.

The pain of the cross must have been unimaginable, but when you picture Jesus up there, think about what—or who—was on His mind.

You were.

That is what made His suffering worth it all. . .He knew that you would one day come to know Him and spend eternity with Him. And as He thought about you, the decision to give His life was settled. He would lay Himself down for those He loved.

No matter where you are, no matter how broken, how fragile, ask the Lord to perfect His work in you. Ask Him to turn things around—not for your own glory or plan—but for His.

His ways are far superior to ours. Yes, you will still go through seasons of suffering. No doubt you'll cry out, "Why me, Lord?" But remember, there's greater glory on the other side of the pain.

Lord, thank You! You gave everything for me. You knew me—and loved me—thousands of years before I was ever born. Wow! You made Your way up the hill with the cross on Your back, and You did it all for me. I'm so grateful, my unselfish Waymaker! Please perfect me through seasons of suffering, I pray. Amen.

A Big Life

You keep track of all my sorrows. You have collected all my tears in your bottle. You have recorded each one in your book.

Psalm 56:8 nlt

Liza unpacked the box that held her favorite dishes. She lovingly fingered the chipped plate, the one her youngest daughter had always loved. Now that daughter was away at college, and the older daughter was married with a family of her own. And Liza was moving from a big, beautiful home to a tiny apartment. . .alone.

When the news came out about her husband's affair, it shook her to the core. Liza tried to work things out, but his heart just didn't seem to be in it. They went through counseling. She prayed, fasted, even attended a Bible study, all in the hopes of saving the marriage. But, in the end, her husband simply wouldn't give up the other woman. He made his choice. . .and she had no choice. Liza felt completely betrayed.

Brokenhearted, she moved out of the family home so that it could be sold. She had no other options, really. She needed the money the sale would bring. With both kids grown, there would be no child support.

But as she surveyed her teensy-tiny apartment, as she held that chipped plate in her hands, the whole thing felt utterly unfair. And heart-wrenching.

Maybe you've been there. You've been wounded by someone and lost everything as a result of their sin. It's not fair! Now you've given up your big, beautiful life, trading it in for one that doesn't even come close.

Remember, to be healthy in a "small" place is better than to be ill in a big one. And God can still give you a "big" life, even when your physical space is smaller.

Lord, that's what I want. . .a "big" life. I want all that You have to offer. So, I'll keep my perspective where it should be! I won't mourn the "would have, should have, could have" stuff. I'll keep my eyes on You, my Waymaker. You have big things planned for me. I just know it! Amen.

Huffing and Puffing

"Behold, I have refined you, but not as silver; I have tried you in the furnace of affliction."
Isaiah 48:10 ESV

Have you ever read the fable about the three little pigs? That mean old wolf huffed and puffed and tried to blow their house down.

That's how we are sometimes. We face challenges. . .problems so deep they seem unfixable. We grumble. We complain. We pour out our hearts to friends. Like that naughty wolf, we huff and we puff and we do all we can to blow those walls down with our sour attitude.

But the walls remain, stronger and taller than ever! And then we get angry at God because He left them there. He could have stopped the situation, but He chose not to. Why? Doesn't He care? Or is He deliberately letting us down?

This, of course, leads to more whining and complaining.

Here's the truth: All the huffing and puffing won't blow the house down. There's only one way to combat a broken situation: Put your trust in God to battle on your behalf. You can't do this on your own, girl. And all the anger and fussing won't make things better. It will only serve to discourage you.

So, stop that whining. Stop that complaining. Don't grumble over the situation you find yourself in. If you've been angry at the Lord, do your best to get past it. Then, as peace settles into your heart, realize that He's been using this situation (and all that huffing and puffing) to refine you.

Yes, you've been through the fire, but you're coming out on the other side as silver not dross.

Lord, I have to confess. . .I've huffed and puffed. A lot. Thank You for letting me have my pity parties, Father. Help me turn away from the grumbling and complaining. I want to learn to trust You again, to have hope again, and to look forward not backward. I need You, my Waymaker! Amen.

Acquainted with Grief

He was despised and rejected—a man of sorrows, acquainted with deepest grief. We turned our backs on him and looked the other way. He was despised, and we did not care.

Isaiah 53:3 NLT

What an interesting way this verse from Isaiah foreshadows the Messiah: as a man of sorrows, acquainted with deepest grief. These words were written long before Jesus came on the scene, but they rightfully depicted the one emotion he would feel above all others—grief.

Strange, isn't it, that Isaiah chose that one? It really shows us that Jesus can connect with us when we're grieving because He's been there too. Perhaps you know what that feels like. Maybe grief extended its hand and asked you to shake it. You wanted to turn and run, but grief already held you in its grip.

Darlene Deibler Rose was a young American missionary who ministered alongside her husband to the Kapauku people in the mountainous region of New Guinea. When World War II broke out with Japan, they were both taken prisoner and forced into Japanese prison camps, where her husband died. Though she survived, Darlene continued a journey filled with horrors none of us would like to face. She agonized over the grief of losing her husband and suffered the additional anguish caused by her own torture.

When you hear this story, what comes to mind? Would you give up if you were in Darlene's shoes? Can you see that she was "a woman of sorrows, acquainted with grief"? Weren't those the very words used to describe Jesus?

Darlene chose to lay aside any bitterness or pain and deepened her relationship with Jesus. She went on to do great things for Him. He made a way for her—out of the grief, out of the pain, and into many more years of service.

Lord, I've been acquainted with grief. I know what it feels like. You know too. We have that in common. I'm so glad You understand, Jesus. Thank You for helping me take steps out of the grief. I know You have a lot more for me to do, and I don't want to get stuck in the pain. Amen.

And the Walls Fell Down!

Humble yourselves, therefore, under God's mighty hand, that he may lift you up in due time. Cast all your anxiety on him because he cares for you.

1 PETER 5:6–7 NIV

Have you ever been through a season where you let walls go up between you and someone else? It's hard to knock them down once they're firmly planted, isn't it? Sometimes we do the same thing with the Lord—we get upset because He didn't answer our prayers when and how we felt He should, so we put up walls and say, "I'm not speaking to You anymore."

If you've read the Old Testament story of Joshua, you know that he faced a fortified city called Jericho. The walls were huge, and they encompassed the whole town. God instructed Joshua to march with his men around those walls for six days. On the seventh day, they went around and around and around. . .seven times in all! Then they blew their trumpets, and the walls fell to the ground!

Some people believe that the walls fell in such a way that they served as ramps into the city. Wow! The same walls that once separated them from their prize became their way in. That'll preach!

What are the Jerichos in your life? What walled cities are you facing? Do you feel as if the walls will never come down?

Here's the truth: God wants those walls to fall. They're keeping you from all that He has planned for you. It's going to take some effort on your part. You might have to march and blow that trumpet as an act of faith. But if you believe those walls will tumble, they will!

Lord, I can see that I have some walled cities in my life, but I'm going to stand firm and wait for a miracle. Bring those walls down, I pray! Amen.

The Wind of the Spirit

Finishing is better than starting. Patience is better than pride.
ECCLESIASTES 7:8 NLT

Just about the time COVID restrictions lifted in her area and folks were getting back out, Jana tested positive for the virus. She found herself stuck at home alone. As an empty-nest mom, recently divorced, there was no one in the house to tend to her needs, to cook food, to take care of the bills, and so on. She was truly on her own and felt it. . .keenly.

But God provided in other ways. Her grown daughters lived nearby and did an admirable job of dropping off meds and groceries on her back porch table. Friends sent gift cards for food delivery, and many of them checked on her daily. These precious people really lifted her spirits.

When she was finally free to go out, Jana celebrated by spending time with her grandkids. They went for a walk in a nearby park on a day when the breeze was lovely. There happened to be dead leaves covering the ground, and the kids lifted them in the air and watched them float on the breeze. Jana couldn't help but think about those leaves when she got back home—how free and easy they seemed. How they allowed the breeze to lift and move them.

What about you? Are you free and easy, or do troubles bog you down? Do you allow the Spirit of God to lift you above your circumstances, or are you more likely to trudge through them? Do you see how your Waymaker is using others to lift your spirits even now?

Today, give yourself fully to the Lord. Say, "Spirit of God, have Your way! Lift me, move me, fill me, use me!"

Oh, my precious Waymaker! You want to lift me above my circumstances. You've used some precious loved ones to encourage me. And I sense Your Spirit, causing my heart to feel light even during hard times. I give myself to You afresh, ready to float on the wind of the Spirit! Amen.

Give Yourself a Break!

And without faith it is impossible to please him, for whoever would draw near to God must believe that he exists and that he rewards those who seek him.
HEBREWS 11:6 ESV

Mattie filled the holes in the yard where the dog had dug. She grumbled the whole time as she shoveled and packed it into place. It seemed no matter how hard she worked to keep up with him, the dog was always one step ahead of her. Chewing up the TV remote. Shredding her favorite pillow. Biting a hole in her favorite comforter. That dog was a piece of work!

Do you ever wonder if God looks at us like Mattie looked at that dog? Does He grumble and complain and carry on about all our mistakes? Does He grab the shovel and start whacking at the ground, filled with angst?

Never! He loves, He forgives, and He gently fills the holes so that you can't even see they were ever there. Because God knows the truth—we're won by love. And patience. And understanding.

Maybe you haven't been very patient with yourself. It's difficult when you see flaw after flaw. The holes are getting bigger not smaller. The debt is getting deeper. The house is getting messier. The dog is getting naughtier. The frustration is growing exponentially.

Here's the truth: You need to be as kind to yourself as Jesus is to you. No, really. Give yourself a break! Tackle those jobs in a way that makes sense to your schedule. Get organized, but don't get overwhelmed. Ask your Waymaker to help you make a way through those everyday challenges that threaten to rob you of your peace.

Lord, it is the everyday stuff that grates on my nerves sometimes. I need a plan. And energy! Help me find a way through all of the stuff that tries to steal my joy and my peace. Amen.

When Your "Want to" Goes Away

Then Jesus told his disciples a parable to show them that they should always pray and not give up.
LUKE 18:1 NIV

"I'm tired of fighting."

Have you ever used those words? When you're in a lengthy battle (say, a cancer journey or a trek through a difficult marriage), it's easy to want to give up. Let's face it: the human body wasn't meant to keep going 24–7 or to deal with physical pain for long. And the human spirit can only take so much! It's easy to grow weary or to feel like giving up when tribulations drag on and on.

Jesus shared the parable of a very persistent widow who kept going back to the judge to get justice from her adversary. He told His disciples that He was sharing this story to show them that they should always pray and not give up.

Sometimes you must keep going back—again and again and again. It gets old, for sure, but don't give up. No matter how many chemo treatments it takes. No matter how many counseling sessions with that loved one. No matter how many mornings you feel you can't get out of bed.

Get out of bed. Keep going. And going. Don't let the enemy rob you of the fighting spirit. Ask God to pour it out afresh today so that you will stay in the game, no matter how tough.

Lord, sometimes my "want to" goes away. I just feel like giving up! In the moment, it seems easier to give up than to keep fighting. But You won't let me give up, will You? You keep nudging me to put one foot in front of the other, reminding me that You, my Waymaker, will make a way even through situations that drag on for ages. Give me patience, I pray! Amen.

A Hankerin' for More

And now, dear brothers and sisters, we want you to know what will happen to the believers who have died so you will not grieve like people who have no hope.

1 THESSALONIANS 4:13 NLT

Debbie had a craving. She wanted a steak. A big, juicy steak, medium, with a baked potato and a salad. She tried to talk her husband into going to their favorite local steakhouse, but he responded with the words, "In this weather? I really don't want to go out."

So, they didn't. Instead, she made spaghetti for dinner. Only, it wasn't steak. So, that spaghetti didn't quite hit the spot. It didn't even come close, in fact. She grumbled about it as she washed the dishes afterward.

Maybe you've been there. You've had a craving for something, and nothing else would do. Only, you never seemed to fill the hole.

There's a God-shaped hole in your heart, and it's meant only for Him. You can fill it with friends, entertainment, food, sex, or any other habits you might choose; but that original "hankering" won't go away because the Lord put it there. He's wooing you to Himself, and anything else you chase after won't come close.

There's nothing like the real deal. Go get the steak. And go deep with God. When you're walking with the one and only true Creator, nothing else will do. You might not notice in the good times, but during hard seasons, you'll realize you've been falling for a counterfeit.

Lord, today I'm chasing after only You! Nothing else will do! I want the whole steak platter! I want to see You move in my life, but more than that. . .I want intimate times of refreshing with You, my Waymaker. So, I run to You today, knowing I will find all I need and more. Amen.

Letters from Home

Since, then, you have been raised with Christ, set your hearts on things above, where Christ is, seated at the right hand of God.
Colossians 3:1 NIV

"The Holy Scriptures are our letters from home."

St. Augustine of Hippo painted such a lovely image with these words. When you've been away from home for months at a time, a letter can be a lifeline. It's a reminder of your roots, where you're loved, accepted, wanted. And it's a reminder of that which is to come, hope for the future.

That's what the Bible is for us as believers. . . our letters from home. It's our lifeline. It's the one thing that brings hope when nothing else does. When we've forgotten where we came from, why we're here, or where we're going, those letters from our Waymaker bring everything back into perspective again.

He's really got a way with words too!

Perhaps you're going through a season where your thoughts continually replay the broken images from yesterday. You think you can't get past it. What you need, sweet friend, is a letter from home. You need to hear from your Daddy. You need a reminder that you are loved, that you have value, and that things really will get better.

Today, take the time to read those letters. Dig into the inspired words from the Bible that can transform not just your situation but you, personally. Read them as gospel truth. Then allow them to change your thinking.

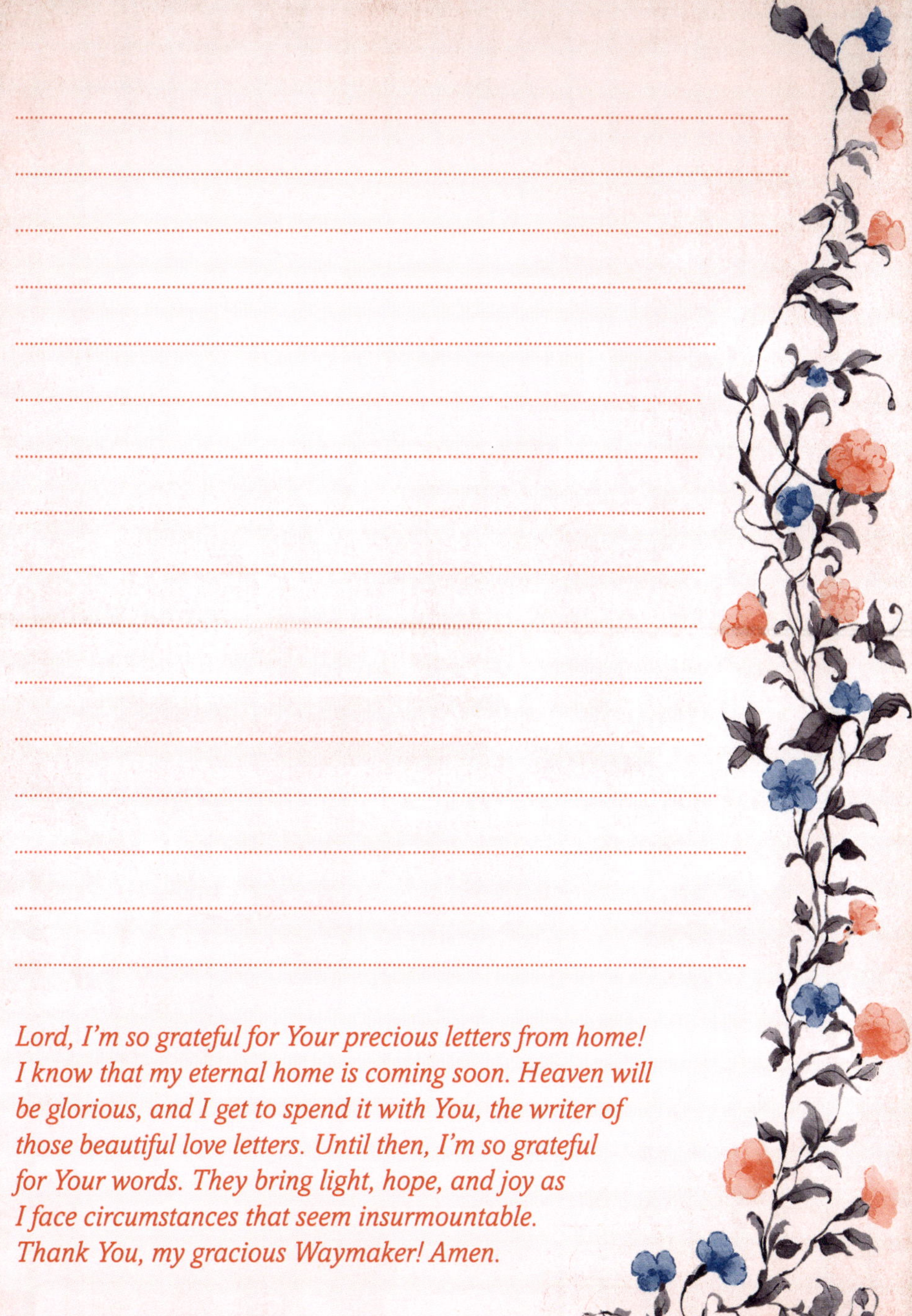

Lord, I'm so grateful for Your precious letters from home! I know that my eternal home is coming soon. Heaven will be glorious, and I get to spend it with You, the writer of those beautiful love letters. Until then, I'm so grateful for Your words. They bring light, hope, and joy as I face circumstances that seem insurmountable. Thank You, my gracious Waymaker! Amen.

The Best Lifeguard Ever

Fear not, for I am with you; be not dismayed,
for I am your God; I will strengthen you, I will help you,
I will uphold you with my righteous right hand.

Isaiah 41:10 ESV

Nora made her way into the pool with her four-year-old daughter in her arms. The youngster wanted to swim but was afraid of the water. Nora spent the next hour gently instructing her until little Brooke finally overcame her fears. Finally! She got the knack of pulling her arms through the water in long strokes and keeping her head afloat at the same time. Her technique wasn't perfect, but she made progress. And they would keep working on it until Nora felt confident her daughter really had the ability to save herself, should the situation arise.

After they finished, Nora celebrated her daughter's victory with ice-cream sundaes. She could hardly wait to tell her husband that their little girl was a swimmer. . .a real swimmer!

Maybe you've been in a situation where you wondered if you could keep your head above water. Sometimes you feel like you're sinking, going under fast. The mortgage company isn't willing to work with you. You've gotten a bad diagnosis from the oncologist. Your car won't start. The boss is calling. . .at midnight. On and on it goes in a never-ending cycle.

When these things pile up, it can feel like you're drowning. That's exactly how the enemy of your soul—that sneaky devil—wants you to feel! He'll do everything he can to pull you under.

Oh, but you have a Waymaker, and He's the best lifeguard ever! He's ready to dive head-first into the deep end of the pool and pull you out. He wants you to call out to Him today, to ask for His intervention in the things that are weighing you down. You don't have to deal with them alone. He's right there, ready to lift you above those circumstances.

Thank You, my precious Waymaker, for lifting my head so that I can breathe! I do feel like I'm drowning at times. But You're truly a Lifeguard, one who guards my life, my heart, and my spirit. How I praise You, Lord! Amen.

The Tow Truck Is Coming

"Let not your hearts be troubled.
Believe in God; believe also in me."
JOHN 14:1 ESV

"Don't worry about it!" Melissa could almost envision her grandfather's thick Italian accent as his favorite phrase flitted through her mind.

Only, she had to worry about it. With her car broken down on the side of the road, what else could she do?

She pushed open the door, doing her best to avoid the traffic barreling down the road next to her. When Melissa stepped outside, she wasn't sure what her next move should be. Pop the hood? She knew nothing about what was inside, so what would that help?

Thank goodness, a truck pulled up behind her. A tow truck. Talk about divine intervention! Was her Waymaker looking on, perhaps? Had He already made provision, even before she asked?

Minutes later, the car was on the truck and headed down the road toward the repair shop.

Did you ever think about the fact that God already has a solution in mind before we've diagnosed our problems? The tow truck is already on the road. It's already headed our way, ready to lift us up and transport us.

That's because your Waymaker is a "behind the scenes" God. He's getting everything in place for the miracles yet to come. He's coordinating everything perfectly. Those times when it feels like things come together seamlessly? A lot of effort has gone into those moments, and all in advance from your great Waymaker!

Think about the many times He has intervened in your life. Consider the timing. Did God already have the players in place? Were the pieces of the puzzle already coming together in such a way that He simply needed to slip the last one in so the picture was complete?

He thinks of everything! Even now He's preparing for circumstances ahead. Don't worry! The tow truck is coming!

Lord, You're always one step ahead of me! You have me covered even before I realize I need covering. How grateful I am. Amen.

Rushing to Save

We know what real love is because Jesus gave up his life for us. So we also ought to give up our lives for our brothers and sisters. If someone has enough money to live well and sees a brother or sister in need but shows no compassion—how can God's love be in that person? Dear children, let's not merely say that we love each other; let us show the truth by our actions.

1 John 3:16–18 NLT

We've all heard those horrible stories about bad guys stealing cars with babies inside. Maybe Mama got out to fill the gas tank, walked around to the other side of the car, and the thief hopped in the driver's seat and took off, never knowing there was a child inside with him.

Picture that mother running down the street, flagging other cars to give chase. She won't relent until that baby is back in her arms again. Nothing can stop her as she races down the road—no traffic, no obstacle, no weather crisis. She's solely focused on one thing—her child.

There's nothing like a crisis to bring out those maternal feelings, is there? Thank goodness most of those stories end well, with the bad guy getting caught and the baby returned safely to his mother. But that mama? She'll never stop watching, guarding, and protecting that child. From that moment on, she'll be a true "helicopter" mom, hovering close.

God is like that mother, relentless in His pursuit when the enemy attempts to drag you away. He flags down every person—or situation—He can find to bring you back. He won't stop until you're safely in His arms once more. And nothing will stop Him—no plan of the enemy, no arguments from you, no natural disaster. He's going to chase you down until you're tucked away under His wing once more.

Thank You for rushing in to save me, my Waymaker! Nothing stops You from pursuing me. I know it's Your great love that propels You to give chase. Thank You for loving me enough to bring me home again. Amen.

The Brightest Star of All

A joyful heart is good medicine,
but a crushed spirit dries up the bones.
PROVERBS 17:22 ESV

Think of the most famous person you know. Maybe it's a president or a king. Maybe it's a Hollywood star or an uber-talented musician from Nashville. Perhaps it's someone who's deeply spiritual—a pastor or a missionary. Or even your best friend!

Different people garner accolades for a variety of skills and accomplishments, but none of them—even the most talented—can come close to doing what the Lord can do. He's more marvelous than all of them put together, and He's always thinking of you, His beloved daughter. Think about it:

They can't pull you from the pit.

They can't walk you through the fire.

They can't guide you through the storm.

No person, no matter how famous, can truly guide you through the broken seasons.

Only one can do all of that, and He often goes unnoticed. Even though He spun the galaxies into existence, He's often overlooked.

Your Waymaker is the most remarkable of them all! His gifts are lifesaving, majestic, and eternal! They defy explanation and cause onlookers to marvel. No doubt He's wishing more people would notice, instead of looking to Hollywood, the music industry, or even pulpits for their superstars.

He's the brightest star of all. He lights up the night skies in magnificent splendor and points the way to an eternal destiny with Him.

Today, take the time to thank your precious Waymaker for the many, many ways He shines bright in your life.

Lord, I won't look to anything or anyone but You. Nothing comes close! Only You can rescue me from danger. Only You can pull me from the pit. You've guided me through hundreds of storms and have crossed deserts to find me when I wandered. No one cares for me like You, Jesus. How grateful I am! Amen.

His Nurturing Nature

"I have said these things to you, that in me you may have peace. In the world you will have tribulation. But take heart; I have overcome the world."

JOHN 16:33 ESV

Gillian was a real softie, especially where animals were concerned. She fostered for a local shelter and never met a dog she didn't like. Some would say she had a nurturing nature. It was just part of her DNA to care about the needs of pups who had no one else to fight for them. Gillian was particularly drawn to the ones that no one else wanted—the sick, the elderly, those with disabilities. Her heart would latch on to them every time.

One day, while helping at the shelter, she happened upon an older dog—blind and deaf, shaking in a kennel. The poor thing had an upper respiratory infection and was in rough shape. She couldn't help herself. Gillian took that dog home and nursed her back to health.

It wasn't easy—and it took a lot of time and effort—but eventually the sweet old dog recovered and adapted to Gillian's home. She lived out her days in that safe place.

In so many ways, God is like that wonderful foster parent. He has the best nurturing nature ever! He sees us in our broken state and pours every effort into our full recovery. And though we might come to Him deaf and blind (spiritually speaking), that doesn't stop Him from seeing our potential. When He looks at us, He sees us healed, whole, and loving our new "digs" in heaven.

Even now, your Waymaker is loving you, nurturing you back to health—spiritually, physically, and emotionally. Allow Him to do His perfect work in you today.

Thank You for taking the time and energy to see me past my blindness, Lord. . .the times I refused to see. And thank You for continuing to whisper "I love you!" into my ear, even during those rebellious seasons when I don't want to listen. You've always been right there, loving me and tending to my every need. How grateful I am, my Waymaker! Amen.

Give It Back

"I will give you back your health and heal your wounds," says the Lord. "For you are called an outcast—'Jerusalem for whom no one cares.' "

Jeremiah 30:17 NLT

Remember, when your kids (or grandchildren, nieces or nephews) were young, how you grounded them from the television or video games? Or maybe you had to take away a cell phone or tablet from an unruly kiddo. You take that electronic device, place it on a shelf, and give the disobedient one time to think about what he's done.

There usually comes a point when you relent and return the device. In that moment, as the great exchange takes place, a new bond forms between you and that child.

Now think of all the times the enemy has attempted to steal from you—your health, your finances, your joy, even your relationships. He swipes those things and tries to put them up high, on a proverbial shelf. But Jesus—who's much taller and stronger—comes along and snatches back what rightfully belongs to you. He says, "I'm giving these back now!" And He tosses them straight back into your lap and says, "Hang on tight to those. And keep your eyes wide open so that he doesn't get his sticky fingers on them next time!" Be on guard! You see how he operates.

The Lord loves you so much that He rights the wrongs. He heals the broken. He restores the very things that seem impossible to restore. And He intervenes when the enemy tries to rob you of your joy, your peace, and your zeal for life.

What an amazing Waymaker, to rush to your rescue! He restores what the enemy has stolen!

You've restored my life, Father! You've given back what the enemy stole from me. He tried to take years off my life. He attempted to steal my joy. But You, my precious Waymaker, wouldn't let him. I love Your restoration plan. It's the best. I'm so grateful that You returned to me what was rightfully mine. How I praise You! Amen.

He Will Use You

For he is our God. We are the people he watches over, the flock under his care.

Psalm 95:7 NLT

God often places us strategically to minister to those who are broken and/or alone. Consider the story of Mother Teresa, a humble nun who ministered to street children in Calcutta, India. Instead of a comfortable, cozy life, she gave her all for the cause of those who had nothing.

Stop to think about that for a moment. She didn't have to go to India. Teresa could have chosen a different location, a different situation. She could have opted for a cozy convent in the countryside, far from the hustle and bustle of Calcutta. But when presented with the option, she chose the street children. And there she remained, all her life, pouring herself out on behalf of those precious little ones. She loved God fully, totally, completely—as was demonstrated in how she loved others. For this love, she is remembered and admired.

Maybe you're the sort of person who pours herself out too. You give and give and then give some more. Nothing brings you more joy than touching others with the love of Jesus. Oh, how you love to be used by Him.

He loves it too! And He will use that difficult road you've walked to minister to many.

You might be standing on a mountaintop right now, or you might be knee-deep in a trash heap in a third-world country. Regardless, God will use you if you say, "Father, I'm Yours!" Your Waymaker didn't bring you all this way so you could sit in front of the television and eat bonbons! He has work for you to do!

Lord, I get it! You've delivered me, healed me, and given me a desire to reach others who are hurting. I want to be like Mother Teresa, pouring myself out for those in need. Point me in the right direction, I pray. Amen.

Can't Feel Past It

"He feels only the pain of his own body, and he mourns only for himself."
JOB 14:22 ESV

Perhaps you've heard the expression "She couldn't see past it." There really are situations that are difficult to see past. There are also situations—particularly health-related or emotionally devastating relational breakups—where you can't seem to "feel" your way past it. When you're struggling with an ongoing health crisis, for instance. Or when you've lost a loved one and your heart is so broken you think, "There's no way I'll ever 'feel' normal again."

Then, miraculously, God intervenes. It doesn't happen in an hour. It doesn't happen in a day. But slowly, like a flower bud opening on a dewy morning, those petals begin to push back, to ease their way open. They drink in the sunshine and say, "Oh! There *is* life on the other side!"

Before long, you're feeling more like your old self again or perhaps a new version of your old self. It's not exactly the same, but the sun is still rising every morning. People are still in their cars, headed to the store and to work. And you? You're finally able to put one foot in front of the other because you've finally concluded that you will make it.

You will feel past the situation you're facing at this very moment. Someday. Until you do, don't let those feelings take the reins of your life. They are, after all, just feelings.

Valid? Yes.

Permanent? No.

Lord, thank You for the reminder that I'm not ruled by my feelings. I'm so grateful hard seasons don't last forever, though they often feel like they might. Things do get better. You're making a way past my brokenness even now. And, as the sun rises each new morning, I want to rise too. With Your hand in mine, I can see that as a real possibility. Amen.

Bittersweet Memories

Not only that, but we rejoice in our sufferings, knowing that suffering produces endurance, and endurance produces character, and character produces hope, and hope does not put us to shame, because God's love has been poured into our hearts through the Holy Spirit who has been given to us.

ROMANS 5:3–5 ESV

"No!" Coral let out a cry as the beautiful porcelain doll hit the floor. "Oh, Buddy! How could you?"

She continued to scold the feisty canine as she swept up the broken shards of ceramic from the doll's delicate face. Tears tumbled down her cheeks as bittersweet memories took hold of her heart. Coral remembered visiting her grandmother as a little girl, playing with this gorgeous porcelain doll. She had memorized every feature. In her mind, this doll represented everything that was good and right about her past—a loving family she'd now lost, a home she'd once enjoyed.

And now it was gone, broken slivers in a wastebasket.

In many ways, Coral's story reminds us that sometimes all we have are our memories. Relationships end. Loved ones pass on. And we feel like we're left sweeping up the crumbs, awash with tears as we drown our sorrows. Situations can feel as hopeless as what Coral faced. And it's easy to blame others when, in reality, some things just happen. They are beyond our control.

Remember, God is still at the helm, even when we feel He's not. It might seem He's stepped away from the scene, but He never does. And don't ever forget that the memories don't have to go away just because the "thing" does. Also keep in mind that your Waymaker is creating new memories even now.

Memories can be lovely things, Lord. I have some beautiful ones from my childhood, and they're often wrapped up in the "items" I've held on to. Thank You for the reminder that You're creating new memories even now. I want to keep my eyes open so that my children, grandchildren, nieces, nephews, and friends will have beautiful memories of me to take with them on their journey. Amen.

The Whole World Is Against Me

What shall we say about such wonderful things as these?
If God is for us, who can ever be against us?
ROMANS 8:31 NLT

Maybe you've spoken these words: "The whole world's out to get me! I just can't win!" There are seasons when it feels that way, for sure. No matter what you do, no matter where you go, things just don't seem to work out. You try and try, but nothing comes together.

Why? Was it something you did? Are you being punished? Or is the world just conspiring against you, determined to keep you down?

Here's a remarkable truth—even if the whole world happened to be out to get you, God would still be for you. If they were chasing you down, He would step in and protect you.

That's amazing, isn't it? Every person, every government, every force of nature on the planet could turn against you, and the Lord of heaven and earth would still be on your side.

And He would be enough.

He would be enough to turn the tide against the attacks of the enemy.

He would be enough to restore your hope and cause you to believe again.

He would be enough to bring new dreams, new visions, and new ideas.

And He would bring a song of praise to your lips right there, in the very middle of the pain.

The next time you feel the world is out to get you, just remind that world who created it. The almighty author and Creator of all is your personal Waymaker, and He has your back!

Lord, I know the world's not really out to get me, though it feels that way sometimes! I go through rough seasons when I feel alone. But with You on my side, I'm never truly alone. Thank You for that reminder today, Father. Amen.

Mercy Triumphs over Judgment

Judgment without mercy will be shown to anyone who has not been merciful. Mercy triumphs over judgment.

JAMES 2:13 NIV

Sometimes you just want to give someone a piece of your mind, don't you? When a neighbor kid hurts your child or someone lashes out at you without provocation, you want to lash right back. It's tempting to hand out justice without mercy, but that was never God's way. He's a God of justice, but He's also merciful and loving.

Perhaps that's why He told us to forgive as many as seventy times seven. Maybe He was trying to say, "Do you get it? There's more to it than just shrugging and saying it's over. It's about learning to care about the other person along the way and saving the relationship when you can."

Justice without mercy is winning for the sake of winning. Justice with mercy is about building relationships. And Jesus is all about relationships.

With all of that in mind, who would you lash out at if you could? Take that person or persons who came to mind and ask God to show you how to love them. . .really, truly love them with His kind of love. Commit to praying for that person not just today but for days and even weeks to come.

Here's the thing: When you add someone to your prayer list, it's hard to be angry at them. Before long, you find yourself praying for their health, their well-being, their finances, and all good things. This is how you love that person the way God loves—by wishing them the best, despite their flaws.

Didn't Jesus forgive you for your mess-ups? Did He wait until you realized what you'd done, admitted it, and begged for forgiveness? No. When He died on the cross, He covered everything you might ever do.

He asked only that you accept His gift and make Him Lord of your life, turning from your sin out of great love for Him.

Your Waymaker will make a way through rough relationships if you learn to love as He loves. Just remember that mercy always triumphs over judgment.

Lord, thank You for the reminder that I need to forgive as You forgive. You pour out mercy not judgment. I want to love as You love, Jesus! Amen.

Stronger Than You Think

Now the Lord is the Spirit, and where the Spirit of the Lord is, there is freedom.
2 CORINTHIANS 3:17 ESV

Have you ever seen a power team perform? They're crazy-strong! They can crack bricks with their foreheads, knock down walls with a swift kick, and lift weights that would send a normal human tumbling to the ground. That kind of supernatural strength doesn't happen overnight. It's slowly built as they lift more, hit harder, and build muscles to accomplish the near-supernatural tasks before them.

When you're in a rough season, it might feel like you have no strength at all. You couldn't smash a bug, let alone a brick. You assume "I'm weak. I can't handle this."

But you might just surprise yourself. Maybe you've been memorizing scriptures or singing worship songs in the weeks or months leading up to this weak moment. At just the right time—when you're in bed with the flu, for instance—a familiar chorus or verse floats through your mind, and you're temporarily transported into God's presence. Suddenly, it all comes back to you—the uplifting words, the joy, the promise that He's right there with you.

It's never too late to beef up, girl! Get those muscles ready now, while things are going well. Memorize those verses. Sing those hymns. Praise at the top of your lungs with those worship songs. You're going to need those promises later.

And remember, even at your very weakest, God is still strong. If He can knock down the walls of Jericho with just a trumpet's blast and a shout of praise, imagine what He can do with your situation.

Lord, You're right there, ready to make a way through my weak moments. When I think I can't. . .You can! When I think I'm too weak, You remind me—through verses, songs, and conversations with friends—that You're plenty strong enough for both of us. Thank You, my Waymaker! Amen.

Stay Plugged In

I know your deeds, your love and faith, your service and perseverance, and that you are now doing more than you did at first.

REVELATION 2:19 NIV

Alix was diagnosed with systemic lupus when she was in her twenties. Her health struggles continued for many years, but she did her best not to let them take her down. All the while, she continued to volunteer at her church, pouring herself out on behalf of others. Even when it made no sense, she wanted to be there, serving little ones at VBS, helping in the kitchen at women's events, handing out bulletins on Sunday mornings.

Being a part of something important was critical to Alix's survival. If she pulled away, if she ostracized herself, she would wither. She would give up. But when she stayed plugged in, she had a support system nearby. She also had joy in her heart as a result of her participation in these wonderful things.

Maybe you can relate. You're in a season where you're feeling a little withered. Perhaps it's because you've stepped away from your church family or from loved ones. You've done so out of necessity—health reasons, pandemic lockdowns, and so on. But you're feeling the effects of trying to walk this road alone.

It's time to reconnect! Your Waymaker never intended for you to do life alone. He's placed you in the body of Christ for a reason. You might be a hand. Or a foot. But you need the rest of the body to be fully functional. And you'll feel better when you're plugged in, so don't pull away unless you have no other choice. Even if you're in a position where you can't actively participate, you can still stay connected through technology.

Lord, thank You for giving me people. And projects. And ministry opportunities. No matter what shape I'm in, I want to stay plugged in, because these wonderful people are a lifeline. I'm so grateful for the family of God! Amen.

He Never Changes

Jesus Christ is the same yesterday and today and forever.
HEBREWS 13:8 NIV

Have you ever had a friend or loved one whose flaws or choices troubled you? Maybe he had a habit that grated on your nerves. Or maybe she had a problem with alcohol and couldn't seem to stop. Maybe he had anger issues. Perhaps she was a shopaholic. You were right to be concerned. After all, these erratic actions affected many people.

Here's a sad truth: Some people just don't seem to change, no matter how many years go by or how many opportunities they're given to turn things around. They selfishly move forward with their own lusts and desires leading the way. They get what they want because they want it. And no one can convince them to change anything.

Here's a really fascinating notion: We can try all day long to make someone change, but the decision is up to them. We can't force them to see the light.

That said, we all know that change *is* possible. If you put your mind to it, you can—and do—change. Alcoholics lay down the bottle. Anger issues are diffused. Drug addicts get delivered from their addiction. Thieves stop stealing. Overeaters find balance. We can change when we give ourselves to the Spirit of God and His transforming power.

Only one never changes, and we wouldn't want Him to. God is the same yesterday, today, and forever. He *was* your Waymaker, He *is* your Waymaker, He *will continue to be* your Waymaker. There's nothing you could ever do or say to stop Him from caring for you.

And because God never changes, you know He's trustworthy. You can count on Him in any situation. Whether you're walking through a valley or soaring over a mountaintop, He's right there, solid as a rock.

Thank You, my precious Waymaker, for never changing! I know I can trust You to stick with me. Nothing I can do will ever drive You away. How I praise You for Your consistent love, Father! Amen.

They're Not Listening to Me

But God has surely listened and has heard my prayer. Praise be to God, who has not rejected my prayer or withheld his love from me!
Psalm 66:19–20 NIV

Have you ever been in a situation where you felt like your voice simply wasn't being heard? Perhaps you sat in a courtroom, pleading your case, but the judge dismissed you. Or maybe you brought a legitimate accusation against someone at work, only to be ignored or ridiculed by your boss or coworkers. It's hard, isn't it? You're speaking, but they're clearly not hearing you.

Some elderly parents have children who never call. Some children have parents who ignore them. Bosses have employees who won't cooperate, and employees have bosses who don't value their opinions.

The unwillingness to listen—*really* listen—is a common problem. And sometimes those with their fingers in their ears are the people you genuinely care about, the ones who should care most about what you think.

Not being heard can hurt a lot. Don't they value you? Isn't your voice or your opinion important? Judging from their apathetic reactions, what you have to say doesn't matter at all.

You scream a little louder to be heard, but the pain of being ignored just deepens as everyone goes about their way without noticing you. Would a megaphone help?

When you're broken inside, you need someone who will listen. Sadly, the world won't always hear you or respond to you, but God will. His ears are wide open. His heart is wide open. And He's not only listening; He's already putting together a plan of action to lead you past this problem into a better place.

Thank You, Lord, for always hearing me. You think my voice matters. You care about what I have to say. I'm grateful for Your tender, loving responses to me when I call on You. Amen.

He Will Do It Again

Come and hear, all you who fear God;
let me tell you what he has done for me.
PSALM 66:16 NIV

When you have a busted faucet or a leaky tub, who do you call? A plumber. When your lights keep flickering, who do you call? An electrician. When your computer goes out, who do you take it to? A computer tech.

When we have a real problem, we go to the experts, those with proven track records. You wouldn't ask a dentist to fix your transmission, and you wouldn't ask your yard guy to bake your daughter's wedding cake. You go to those with the tried-and-true record when you have a real need.

Your Waymaker has such a record. He's an expert. He should be the first one you call on when you're ill, when you have a need, or when you are in a relational crisis. Why? Because He's proven Himself to you time and time again.

Who saved you the last time you were feeling lost? He did.

Who reached down and rescued you when you struggled with addiction? Your Waymaker did.

Who whispers, "You can do this!" when you feel that you can't? He does.

Here's the best news of all: If He does it once, He can do it again.

Now that's something to shout about!

When you find a great plumber, you tell people. When you locate an excellent electrician, you leave reviews or offer recommendations. When you find a trustworthy mechanic, you spread the word.

Today, God wants you to spread the word that He's trustworthy. He wants everyone to know they can lean on Him, that they don't need to look for answers elsewhere.

Keep your focus on the one who's been there all along, and share the news of all He's done so that others can come to know Him too.

Lord, You'll do it again! All of those amazing things You've already done in my life. . .and You're just getting started. I'll write the best reviews and give the heartiest recommendations. I'll tell everyone I know that You'll never let them down, Father! How grateful I am! Amen.

Consequences

All Scripture is inspired by God and is useful to teach us what is true and to make us realize what is wrong in our lives. It corrects us when we are wrong and teaches us to do what is right.

2 Timothy 3:16 NLT

Most seasons of brokenness are caused by things outside of your control—sickness, death, or the actions of others. But some rough seasons come as a result of incidents you caused yourself. In those cases, the remedy might be a little different.

Consider the story of Jonah. God instructed this Old Testament prophet to go to the town of Nineveh. Why? To tell the people they needed to repent and give up their sinful ways. Jonah wasn't keen on this idea, so he ran. He boarded a ship and headed out to sea. When a horrible storm blew up, the men on board the ship decided Jonah was the reason for the squall, so they tossed him overboard!

Jonah was then swallowed by a giant fish. He spent three days in the belly of that beast. God finally had his attention. Jonah had plenty of time to think through all the things that had led him there.

Maybe you can relate to that part of the story. You've run from God. Running away has caused consequences. You find yourself trapped, much like Jonah. You regret the decisions that led you here, but what can you do now? Actions have consequences. How can you fix what you've broken?

Like Jonah, you might need to go back to point A, to where your heavenly Father gave you instructions that you refused to follow. Repent for your disobedience, and do those things He's instructed you to do. Once you've done business with God, turn your heart toward home.

Remember, God doesn't cease to become your Waymaker just because you caused the problem. He still has a way out for you. Give the situation to Him, and watch Him work it out on your behalf.

Thank You for Your forgiveness, Lord, and for the many times You've rescued me. There have been consequences, but I'm grateful they have led me back to You, my Waymaker! Amen.

Don't Forget to Thank Him!

So if you are suffering in a manner that pleases God, keep on doing what is right, and trust your lives to the God who created you, for he will never fail you.

1 PETER 4:19 NLT

There's a fascinating story in the Gospel of Luke. Jesus and His disciples were headed to Jerusalem when they reached the border of Galilee and Samaria. When they entered a village, ten men with leprosy stood a distance away, which was the custom/law. They cried out, "Jesus, Master, have mercy on us!"

Jesus healed all ten! Right then, right there. Then He instructed them to go to the priest to prove that they were clean, something that had to happen before they would be accepted back into society. When the priest declared them "clean," nine of the men went on their merry way—no doubt ready to see their loved ones. But one came back to Jesus. His heart was so filled with gratitude that he fell to the ground at Jesus' feet and offered thanks for his healing. He shouted, "Praise God!" What's remarkable about this part of the story is that this man wasn't a Jew. He was a Samaritan.

Jesus asked, "Didn't I heal ten men?" He already knew, of course, that there were many others, but they had not returned. "Where are the other nine? Has no one returned to give glory to God except this foreigner?" He then instructed the man to stand and go, saying, "Your faith has healed you."

The Waymaker made a way for those ten men, but only one considered it important to thank Him for what He'd done.

What about you? When God moves on your behalf, do you come back to thank Him or do you go on your merry way? Your Waymaker is deserving of your thanks and your praise. Like the Samaritan, fall at His feet and say, "Praise God!"

Oh, Lord! How many times have You touched my life? And how many times did I return to thank You? I'm sorry for the times I forgot to praise You. Thank You for healing me, my precious Waymaker! Amen.

God Is Here

"Be strong and courageous. Do not be afraid or terrified because of them, for the Lord *your God goes with you; he will never leave you nor forsake you."*

Deuteronomy 31:6 niv

Perhaps you've heard of William Cary. He was known as "the father of modern missions" for his missionary work in India. His story begins in 1787, when he voiced his belief that all Christians have an obligation to share the gospel around the globe. Apparently, this didn't go over very well with the people he was with. One of them responded, "Young man, sit down. When God pleases to convert the heathen, He will do it without your aid and mine."

Can you imagine? What a shocking response! How would the Church ever grow if all believers felt like this?

Cary had the good sense to ignore this advice. He founded the Baptist Missionary Society a few years later. Unfortunately, he saw no conversions for many years. During that same time period, he lost a son to dysentery, and his wife suffered a deterioration in her mental health.

But check out Cary's response: "This is indeed the valley of the shadow of death to me. But I rejoice that I am here notwithstanding; and God is here."

Jump ahead to 1800: Cary won his first convert to the faith. Over the twenty years that followed, he translated the Bible into dozens of Indian languages and dialects. Wow!

God proved Himself as a Waymaker in Cary's life. Even when he doubted his call as a missionary, the Lord came through for him.

He'll come through for you too. . .no matter how long it takes or how many obstacles are in your path. Remember Cary's words when you're in a season of brokenness: "This is indeed the valley of the shadow of death to me. But I rejoice that I am here notwithstanding; and God is here."

God, You are here! You will never leave me or forsake me. Even in my seasons of brokenness, You will remain right by my side. How I praise You. Amen.

But You Are Near, O Lord

They draw near who persecute me with evil purpose; they are far from your law. But you are near, O Lord, and all your commandments are true.

Psalm 119:150–151 ESV

When you think about John the Baptist, what comes to mind? Likely your thoughts shift to that remarkable day when he baptized his cousin, Jesus, in the Jordan River. Or maybe you think of him in the wilderness dressed in camel's hair and living on locusts and honey, preparing the way for the Lord.

These are all the usual things people think of when John the Baptist comes to mind; they are incidents that took place at the front end of his life. But he went through seasons of great pain and persecution toward the end of his life, and we would be remiss if we overlooked them.

John had no problem calling people out for their sin, including the king. Because of his boldness, John was arrested and tossed into a prison cell. In a rather bizarre story, the daughter of the king asked for the head of John the Baptist on a platter, and her father obliged. And so, the man who was the forerunner of Christ, the one chosen by God to introduce the world to the Savior, was put to death in a horrific way.

You might read this story and think, "Where was the Waymaker?" Jesus was John's cousin after all! We don't have answers for why bad things happen to good people, but we do know that John believed in an eternal kingdom. He knew that heaven was waiting for him. He's currently celebrating there. If we could ask him, "Would you do it all again?" no doubt his answer would be a resounding "Yes!"

Maybe you can relate to that last part. If someone were to ask you, "Would you do it all again?" what would you say? Perhaps you would think about how far you've come and how much you've grown. But above all, you would say, "God made a way for me through it all. He never left my side."

He never did. . .and He never will.

You are near, O Lord. Just as You were near John the Baptist, You've stuck close to me even in the darkest hours. How I praise You! Amen.

Welcomed in the Throne Room

On the third day Esther put on her royal robes and stood in the inner court of the palace, in front of the king's hall. The king was sitting on his royal throne in the hall, facing the entrance.

Esther 5:1 niv

Sometimes you have no other choice but to trust God. Such was the case with Esther. A young Jewish woman, she never dreamed of one day becoming queen. But she was chosen by King Ahasuerus for her beauty, and the remarkable story of how God used her to save her people got off to a rolling start.

The problems began when Haman, the king's chief advisor, became offended by Esther's cousin and guardian, Mordecai. Haman went straight to the king and asked that all the Jewish people be killed.

As soon as Mordecai heard this, he told Esther to approach the king and let him know that she was Jewish and then ask that he repeal the order.

Back in those days, no one entered the king's throne room without an invitation. They certainly would never approach the throne! To do so might invite death!

You can imagine how scared Esther was! She asked that the entire Jewish community pray and fast for three days before she went to see the king. They obliged.

Esther garnered her courage and made the move into the throne room, where (thank goodness) she was accepted by her husband, who extended his scepter in her direction. He not only welcomed her; he granted her request. And, as a result, the people of God were saved through her. In an added twist, Haman was put to death.

Here's a lovely takeaway from Esther's story: No matter how bleak things look, you are welcomed in the throne room. Your Waymaker is seated on the throne, scepter extended, happy you have come to Him in good times and bad.

Lord, thank You for welcoming me! I know I'm safe in Your presence. You're my guardian, my protector, and my friend. How I love You! Amen.

What Remains

Cast me not away from your presence,
and take not your Holy Spirit from me.
Psalm 51:11 ESV

Corrie ten Boom was a Christian woman from Holland who was sent to a concentration camp for secretly housing the Jews during World War II. She endured countless hardships in that horrible place but managed to keep believing, trusting, and hoping, even after the death of her precious sister, Betsie. She never gave up on God's promise that He would redeem the situation.

Fifteen days after Betsie's death, Corrie was released. She later learned that her release had been a mistake, a clerical error. Less than a week later, all the women in her age group were put to death in the gas chambers.

Corrie went on to write an amazing book, *The Hiding Place*. She also became a well-loved public speaker, sharing her story across the globe. If she could sit and visit with you today, she would rest her hand on yours and say, "Our Waymaker was right there with me, every step of the way. Never doubt that He's with you too."

She would also say, "Use what remains."

"What remains?" you might ask. "What do you mean?"

After you've come through a tragedy, there is much to process. But there are divine takeaways, lessons you learned from the depths. For Corrie, some of those lessons included God's supernatural provision of vitamins for her sister. Another lesson came from the secret Bible study she held for the prisoners when the guards weren't looking.

For you? Well, only you know! But many, many takeaways have come from your journey already. Like Corrie, you have stories to tell. And how wonderful it is to have a Waymaker who has led you all this way.

Lord, I have plenty of takeaways from the tough experiences I've faced. I've learned so much from the good and the bad. Show me how to use what I've learned to encourage others, I pray. I want to be a witness like Corrie, Father. Amen.

A Different Kind of Peace

"Peace I leave with you; my peace I give to you. Not as the world gives do I give to you. Let not your hearts be troubled, neither let them be afraid."

JOHN 14:27 ESV

Back in the 1960s, flower power children sang songs about peace. In their tie-dyed version, peace would come about when the Vietnam War ended. Only then would chaos cease and the world come together in perfect unity. Or so they said.

A few years have passed since then, and we're still struggling with wars and chaos, so the flower power children didn't exactly get what they were looking for. That's because the kind of peace the world offers is artificial. It's temporary. It's an illusion.

There's a peace that comes from walking with Jesus, and it's the real deal. This supernatural peace can settle deep into your heart, even when you're facing something as big as an internal war or something as disruptive as a broken relationship.

No doubt you've discovered this from your own journey. Even during the low seasons, God, in His miraculous way, penetrated the darkness, wrapped His arms around you, and brought supernatural peace. You couldn't explain how it happened exactly, but you felt His presence in a tangible way at a time when most would be feeling despair.

The reason you've sensed His peace was because He gave it to you, wrapped in ribbons and bows, a special-delivery gift. Jesus told His disciples, "Peace I leave you." It was His parting gift. He added the words, "Not as the world gives do I give to you."

Nothing comes close to what your Waymaker has to offer.

Jesus, I'm so grateful for Your gift of peace, which has sustained me during seasons of brokenness. I won't trust the world's counterfeit version of peace. Why would I, when I have You, the real deal? Thank You, my Waymaker! Amen.

A God of the Miraculous

Jesus, once more deeply moved, came to the tomb.
It was a cave with a stone laid across the entrance.
"Take away the stone," he said.
JOHN 11:38–39 NIV

Is anything too hard for the Lord? In the Old Testament story of Abraham and Sarah, this question came up. Sarah was ninety years old and had not yet had the promise of a child fulfilled. When God told her that she would have a son, she laughed. It seemed impossible at her age. But I'm sure you've realized by now that *nothing* is impossible with our Waymaker! He can make a way even when it seems all hope is gone.

Another "impossible" story took place in the Gospel of John. Jesus came to the tomb of His dear friend Lazarus and was ready and willing to raise him from the dead. No one was laughing that day. There were nothing but tears from all in attendance.

Jesus wept.

There are all sorts of speculations about why He cried, but the point is He was overcome with human emotion. And out of that emotion, deeply moved, He performed a miracle.

Jesus cares about what you're going through. He is emotionally invested. Whether you're waiting to conceive or have reached the opposite end of the journey—you're burying a loved one—He's there and He cares. He still wants to engage with you in the very midst of your pain.

So, laughter or tears, let Him in.

Lord, nothing is impossible for You! You are a God of the miraculous. I can't wait to see what miracles You're going to perform in my situation. Thank You, my Waymaker, for making a way even when all hope seems lost. With You, there is always hope! Amen.

Break Up Your Fallow Ground

*Sow for yourselves righteousness; reap steadfast love;
break up your fallow ground, for it is the time to seek the* Lord,
that he may come and rain righteousness upon you.
Hosea 10:12 ESV

God gives us what we need when we need it. His timing is perfect. Think of a farmer dropping seeds in the ground. He plants cabbage seeds and grows cabbage. He plants lima bean seeds and grows lima beans. When the Lord plants something deep in your heart—forgiveness, for example—that's what grows! You must cultivate it, of course. You need to stay in the Word and absorb as many nutrients (verses) as you can. But your heavenly Father loves you and wants to give you good gifts. . . so forgiveness is yours for the asking.

Before the farmer ever begins to plant the seeds, something important must take place. His actions are described in today's verse from Hosea, where we read: "Sow for yourselves righteousness; reap steadfast love; break up your fallow ground."

These are all gardening/farming terms, aren't they? Sow. (Something a farmer knows a lot about.) Reap. (Harvest time!) And "break up your fallow ground."

What does that last one mean? What is fallow ground?

When the soil becomes overgrown with weeds and thorns, the farmer breaks up the soil, releasing the weeds.

That's exactly what your Waymaker wants to do in your heart, even when you're walking through a season of brokenness. He wants to prepare the soil of your heart so that He can plant seeds of love, peace, joy, mercy, goodness, kindness, and so on.

Remember, whatever the farmer sows, the farmer reaps.

If you prepare your heart so that He can drop those seeds down deep, you'll have a harvest of blessings on the other end of the pain.

Lord, I will allow you to break up the fallow ground of my heart. It's dry, cracked, and filled with useless weeds, but I give it to You afresh so that You can bring forth a harvest in my life. Amen.

The Roller Coaster

"If you then, who are evil, know how to give good gifts to your children, how much more will the heavenly Father give the Holy Spirit to those who ask him!"
LUKE 11:13 ESV

Leigh's life was a bit like a roller-coaster ride. Up one minute, down the next. . .she found herself holding on tight, never knowing what was coming next. About the time she started to relax, the next hit would come. Then, in the middle of the pain, something amazing—like the birth of a grandchild—would happen. Just about the time she lifted up a celebratory shout, an incoming hurricane flooded her home. The inconsistencies made her crazy.

Maybe your life has been a bit like that too. You're up. . .and then you're down. Then you're up again, but you're wondering when someone's going to kick your knees out from behind you. In fact, you've been scared to release a breath because you're so worried about the next hit that might come.

Relax, girl! God wants you to know that He's got you, even on this crazy roller-coaster ride. Today's verse from Luke 11 confirms that your heavenly Father is a giver of good gifts. He's not out to get you. You don't have to be afraid of that next freefall. Yes, there will be twists and turns ahead, but that's part of the excitement—learning how to trust when you can't see what's coming around the bend.

You do trust Him, don't you? He's proven Himself trustworthy with every rise and fall. In the blessings and in the valleys. Have you figured out yet that sometimes the valleys end up being the greatest blessings of all?

When you look back on your life, you'll see that the blessings far outweigh the pain. And honestly? They're that much sweeter *because of* the pain.

Lord, I trust You. . .even with the ups and downs. I can't make sense of it, Father, but I know that You're not out to hurt me. You adore me and have nothing but good gifts for me. What a relief, my precious Waymaker! Amen.

A Broken Record

I pray that God, the source of hope, will fill you completely with joy and peace because you trust in him. Then you will overflow with confident hope through the power of the Holy Spirit.

ROMANS 15:13 NLT

Mention a record player, and kids today probably won't know what you are talking about! They sure won't know a 45 from a 33 1/3. For that matter, they won't know what a cassette player is, either!

Depending on your age, you might have played record albums. If so, you've likely heard the expression "a broken record." Usually, when people use that phrase, they're not really talking about a literal record album. They're talking about a person who keeps going on and on and on. . .like a broken record.

Back in the olden days, if a record album got scratched, the needle would skip over the scratch and repeat that part of the song multiple times until you finally lifted the needle and placed it elsewhere. That's where the phrase "a broken record" came from.

Some people, when they go through pain, are like broken records. They just keep replaying and replaying what happened to them. They don't ever seem to get healed from it. After a while, people wonder if they even want to.

Don't be a broken record. Don't keep replaying and rehearsing what happened to you. As much as you're able, give it to Jesus. He'll guide you through. In doing so, you will be an uplifting testimony to all those who are watching.

Lord, I know that I sometimes replay the negatives. I rehearse them aloud to anyone who will listen. But every time I do that, I end up frustrated all over again. It feels like it's happening afresh. I don't know how You're going to accomplish this, Father, but I ask that You lift this need to replay the story from me. Remove it altogether, I pray. Amen.

All the King's Horses

Though my father and mother forsake me, the Lord will receive me.
Psalm 27:10 NIV

"Not again!" Mandy groaned as she looked inside the egg carton. One of the largest eggs was cracked, and the sticky liquid had oozed out in the carton, gluing the eggshell firmly in place and spilling over onto the next egg. She tried to lift it out, but it broke in her hand and made an even bigger mess. And talk about a smell!

Maybe you've dealt with that same problem. Once an uncooked egg is cracked, it must be used immediately or it spoils in record time. There's no mending it. Like Humpty Dumpty, there's no gluing it back together. All the king's horses and all the king's men can't uncrack it. Cook that egg ASAP. . .or toss it. There are no other options.

Sometimes we feel a bit like a cracked egg. We're broken, only no one seems to notice. They go on about their business without paying attention to our cracks and crevices. Our pain silently seeps out and locks us in place. It causes a stench. The longer we stay in that condition, the worse it becomes. If only we'd fixed the problem right away, then perhaps we could break free.

Here's good news: We have a Waymaker who's really good at putting Humpty Dumpty back together again. What we cannot do, He can.

You're not a cracked egg. You're a precious, holy child of the King of kings. You're loved, adored, and noticed. When you think no one cares about the pain you're in, think again! The Creator of the universe has already stepped into the very middle of your situation and has dispatched an entire angel army to help you through this. That's how much your Waymaker cares.

I'm so glad You were paying attention when I was cracked and broken, Lord. For a while there, it looked and felt hopeless to me. But You're the mender of all things. You put me back together again and set me on a path toward healing. How grateful I am! Amen.

Praise Him in All Circumstances

Give thanks in all circumstances; for this is God's will for you in Christ Jesus.

1 THESSALONIANS 5:18 NIV

There's a marvelous story in the book of Judges about a prophetess named Deborah. She offered counsel to many, including a great military man named Barak. Together, they went to battle against the Canaanites at Mount Tabor. They won that battle because the Lord was on their side. God is on your side too! So, when you face battles, remember that He will fight for you if you allow Him to.

We read in the fifth chapter of Judges that Deborah and Barak offered up a song of praise once their battle was won. Can you imagine how triumphant they must have sounded?

There are lessons in their story. You don't have to wait until the battle is won to praise the Lord, though it's great to praise and thank your Waymaker once He's performed a miracle on your behalf, of course. You can start right now, even when the battle is raging. Sometimes we forget to do this, don't we? We walk through seasons of brokenness and forget about the power of praise.

When you stop to thank God, to lift a song or a word of thanks, your thoughts shift from yourself and the problem to Him. And when your thoughts are on Him, He can transport you far beyond your current reality.

What's stopping you today? Wherever you are in your journey, this is the right moment to praise Him. In the throes of the battle? Praise Him. Looking back on how far He's brought you? Praise Him.

It's always a good day to praise.

Lord, I don't always remember to praise. Some days I get so bogged down, so troubled by the problem, that I forget. Please remind me in the moment! I praise You, my Waymaker! Amen.

All Things

And we know that for those who love God all things work together for good, for those who are called according to his purpose.

Romans 8:28 ESV

All things. The Word of God says your Waymaker will make *all things* work together for good for those who love Him and have His calling on their lives.

Sometimes it's hard to imagine, isn't it? You walk through a season so desperate, so unimaginably hard, and you think to yourself, "How in the world could God possibly work this together for my good?" The situation is too extreme. The outlook is too devastating. All hope is gone. Your proverbial cart has gone off the road, and nothing can bring it back again.

Then, somehow, God begins to do what only He can do. He steps in, takes the reins, and begins to maneuver that cart back toward the center mark once again. And in the process, He sends a gentle reminder that you were never really the one in control, anyway. He was and is.

Do you trust Him? Even now, in the middle of the swirling, whirling mess going on around you? Do you trust that He can, in an instant, intervene and work out this story not just for your good but for His glory?

That's the goal, of course: to exhibit His glory for the world to see. So, watch out, believer! Get ready! He's going to work all things together for the good of those who are called according to His purpose. That's a promise you can take to the bank.

Father, we know You love us. And we're so grateful You take the messes in our lives and use them for Your glory. We offer ourselves—and our situations—to You. We are called to Your purpose and anticipate great things as we walk out that purpose. What a loving Waymaker You are. How we love You! Amen.

Scripture Index

OLD TESTAMENT

NEW TESTAMENT

Journal Your Journey of Faith

Pray More: A Devotional Journal for Women

This delightful devotional journal features daily readings and prayers designed to help you live your best life as you learn to place your trust in the Almighty God, who gives you courage.

Hardback Cloth / 978-1-63609-912-5

Good Morning, God! An Encouraging Prayer Journal for Women

What better way to guarantee a good morning than to spend time in prayer? *Good Morning, God!* encourages you to do just that—to set aside a few minutes each day for quiet time with God. Nearly 200 faith-building devotional prayers are accompanied by inspiring scripture selections and journaling space.

Flexible Casebound / 978-1-63609-848-7